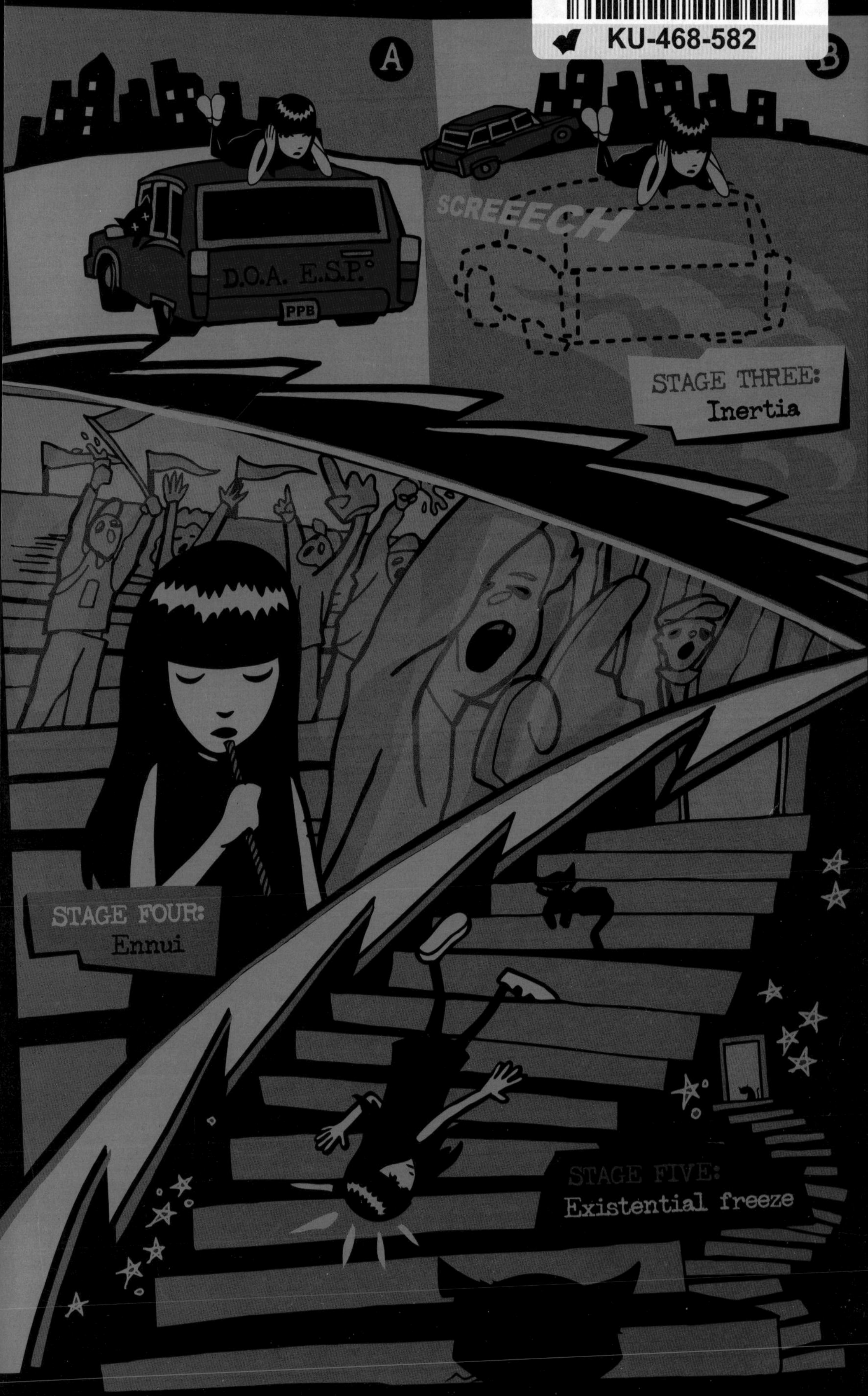
A
B
D.O.A. E.S.P.
PPB
SCREEEECH
STAGE THREE:
Inertia
STAGE FOUR:
Ennui
STAGE FIVE:
Existential freeze

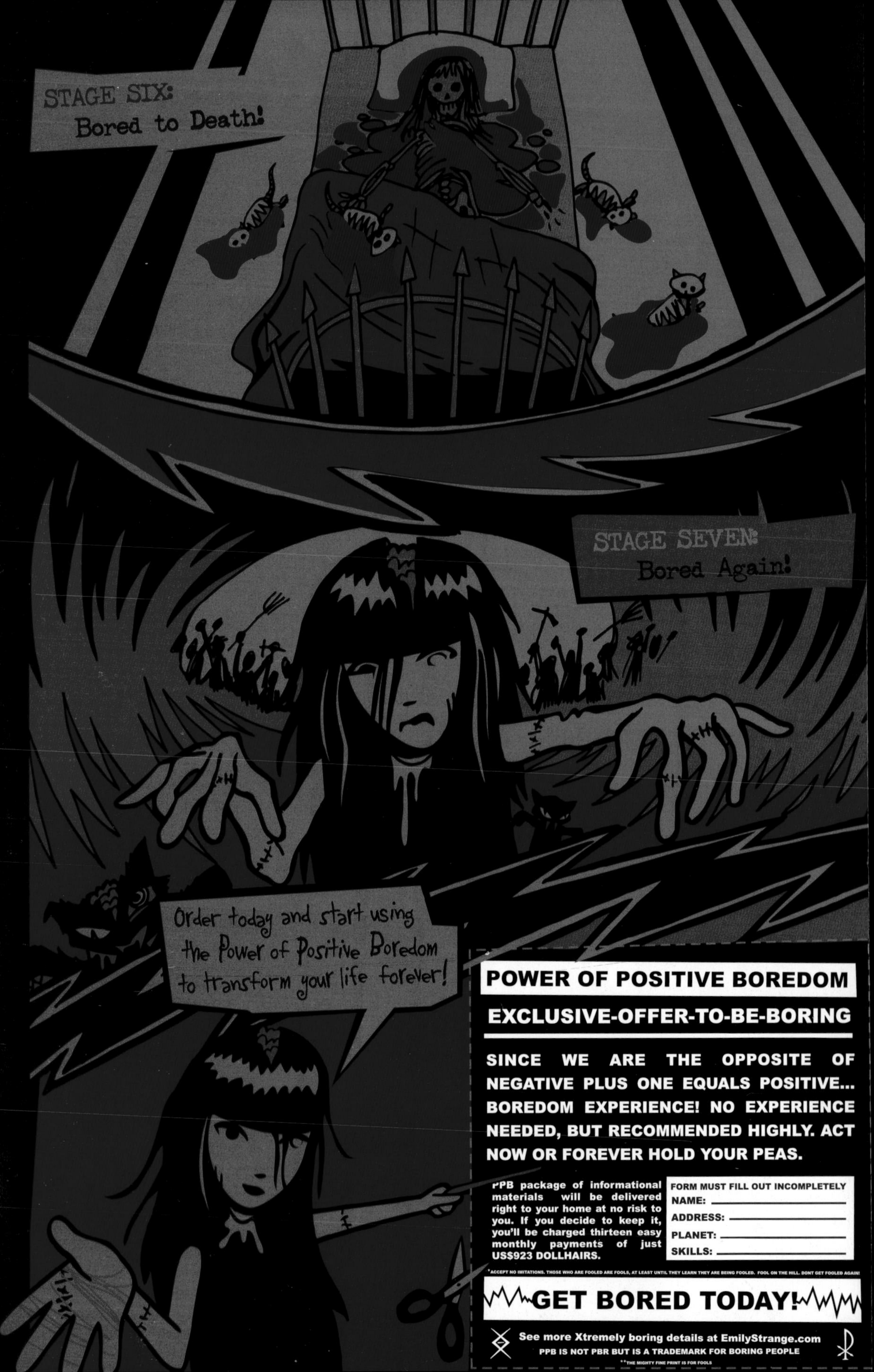

STAGE SIX: Bored to Death!
STAGE SEVEN: Bored Again!
Order today and start using the Power of Positive Boredom to transform your life forever!
POWER OF POSITIVE BOREDOM
EXCLUSIVE-OFFER-TO-BE-BORING
SINCE WE ARE THE OPPOSITE OF NEGATIVE PLUS ONE EQUALS POSITIVE... BOREDOM EXPERIENCE! NO EXPERIENCE NEEDED, BUT RECOMMENDED HIGHLY. ACT NOW OR FOREVER HOLD YOUR PEAS.
PPB package of informational materials will be delivered right to your home at no risk to you. If you decide to keep it, you'll be charged thirteen easy monthly payments of just US$923 DOLLHAIRS.
FORM MUST FILL OUT INCOMPLETELY
NAME:
ADDRESS:
PLANET:
SKILLS:
*ACCEPT NO IMITATIONS. THOSE WHO ARE FOOLED ARE FOOLS, AT LEAST UNTIL THEY LEARN THEY ARE BEING FOOLED. FOOL ON THE HILL. DONT GET FOOLED AGAIN!
GET BORED TODAY!
See more Xtremely boring details at EmilyStrange.com
PPB IS NOT PBR BUT IS A TRADEMARK FOR BORING PEOPLE
**THE MIGHTY FINE PRINT IS FOR FOOLS

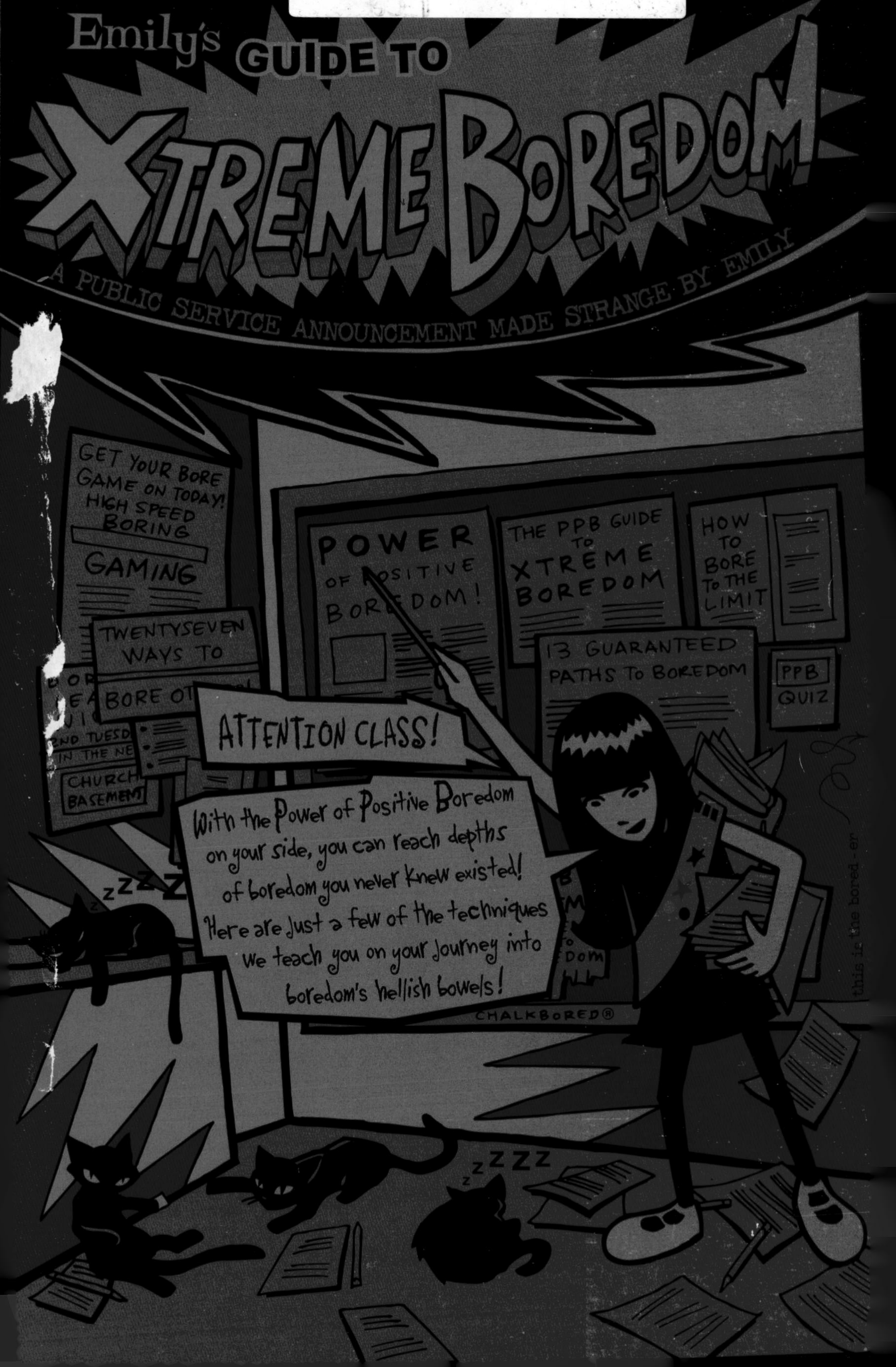
Emily's GUIDE TO
XTREME BOREDOM
A PUBLIC SERVICE ANNOUNCEMENT MADE STRANGE BY EMILY
GET YOUR BORE GAME ON TODAY! HIGH SPEED BORING GAMING
TWENTYSEVEN WAYS TO
2ND TUESD
IN THE NE
CHURCH BASEMENT
POWER OF POSITIVE BOREDOM!
THE PPB GUIDE TO XTREME BOREDOM
HOW TO BORE TO THE LIMIT
13 GUARANTEED PATHS TO BOREDOM
PPB QUIZ
ATTENTION CLASS!
With the Power of Positive Boredom on your side, you can reach depths of boredom you never knew existed! Here are just a few of the techniques we teach you on your journey into boredom's hellish bowels!
CHALKBORED®
ZZZ
ZZZZ
this is the bored-er

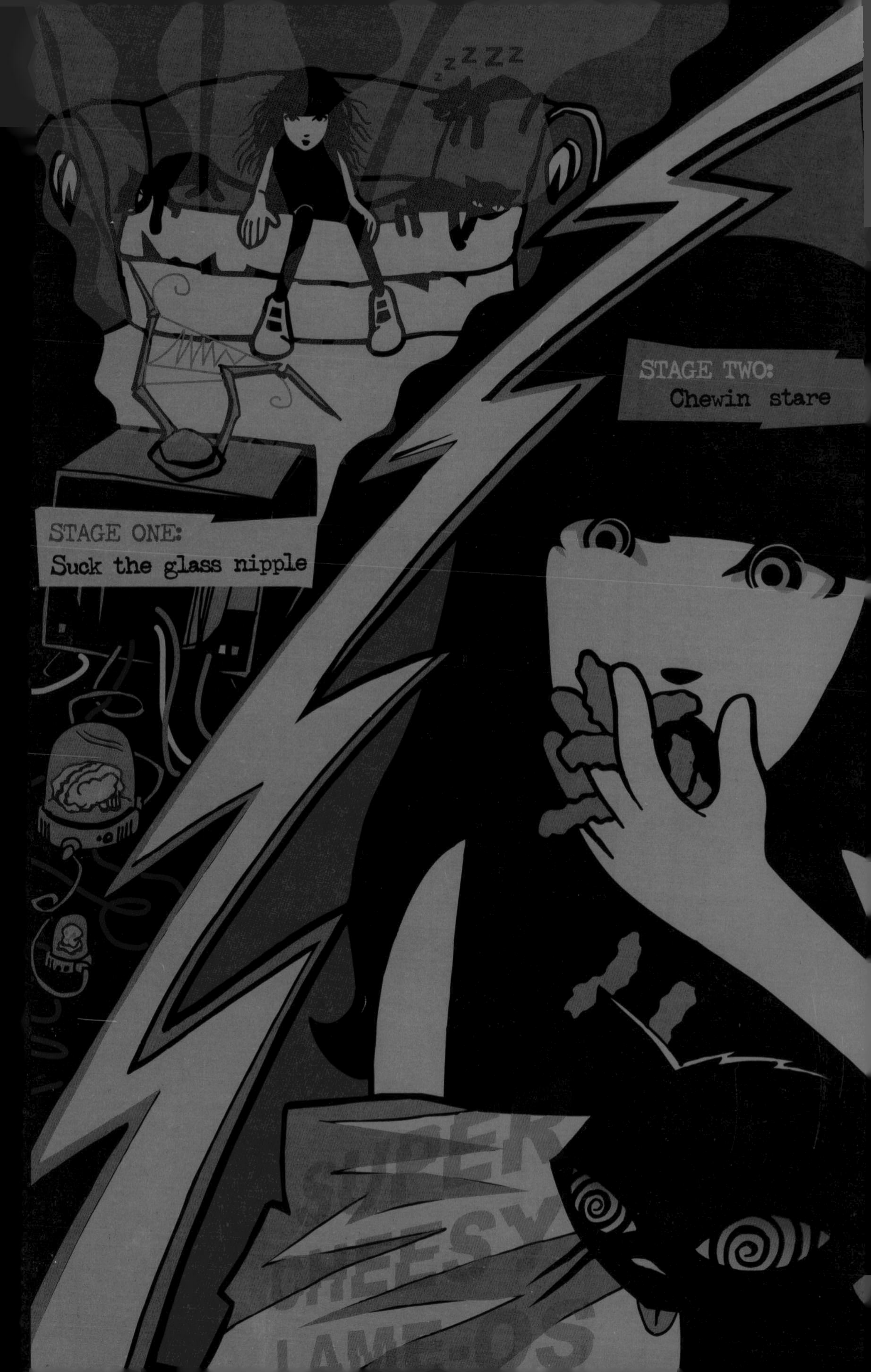
STAGE ONE:
Suck the glass nipple
STAGE TWO:
Chewin stare

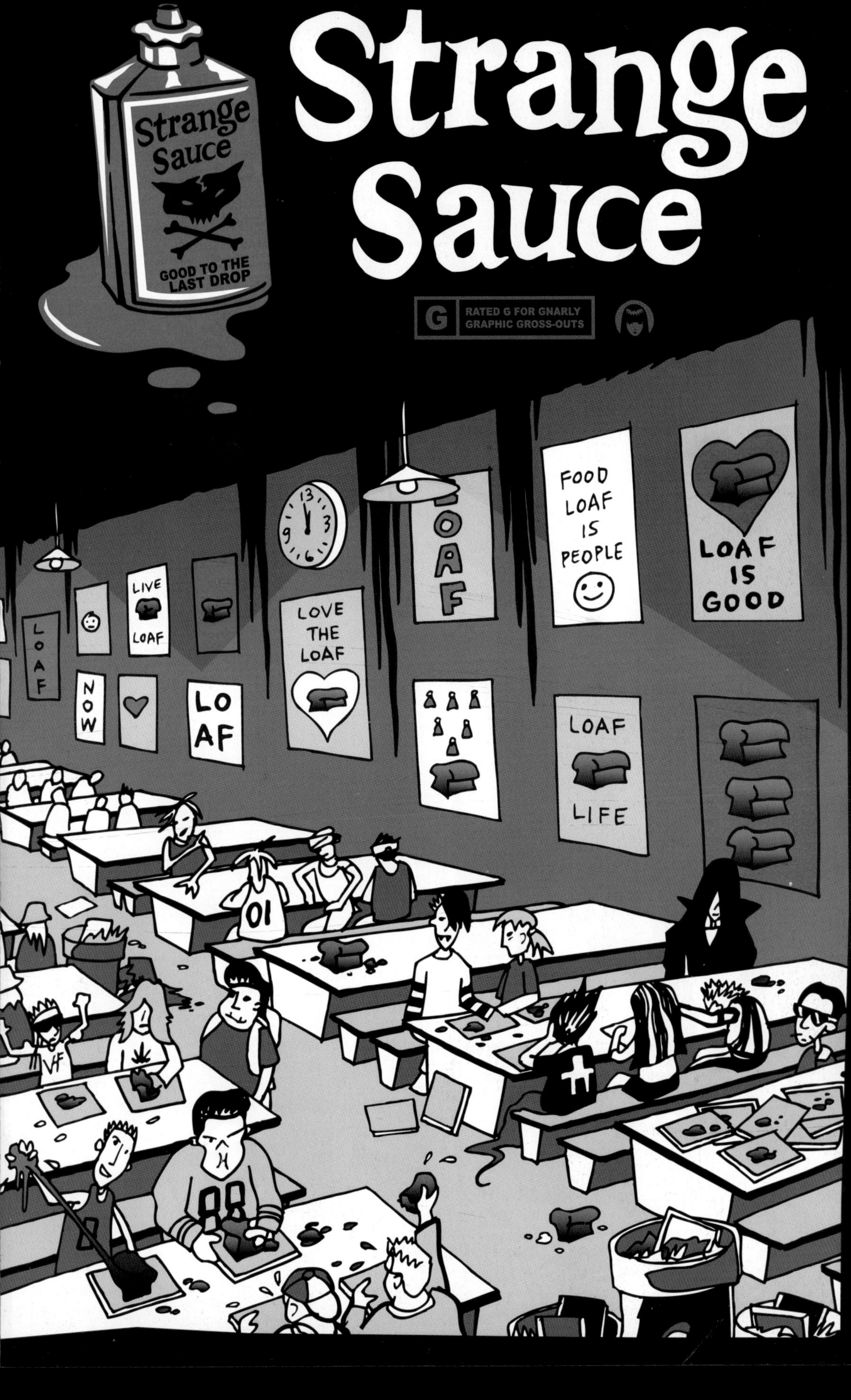
Strange Sauce
Strange Sauce
GOOD TO THE LAST DROP
G
RATED G FOR GNARLY GRAPHIC GROSS-OUTS
FOOD LOAF IS PEOPLE
LOAF IS GOOD
LOAF
LOVE THE LOAF
LIVE LOAF
LOAF
NOW
LO AF
LOAF LIFE
01
88

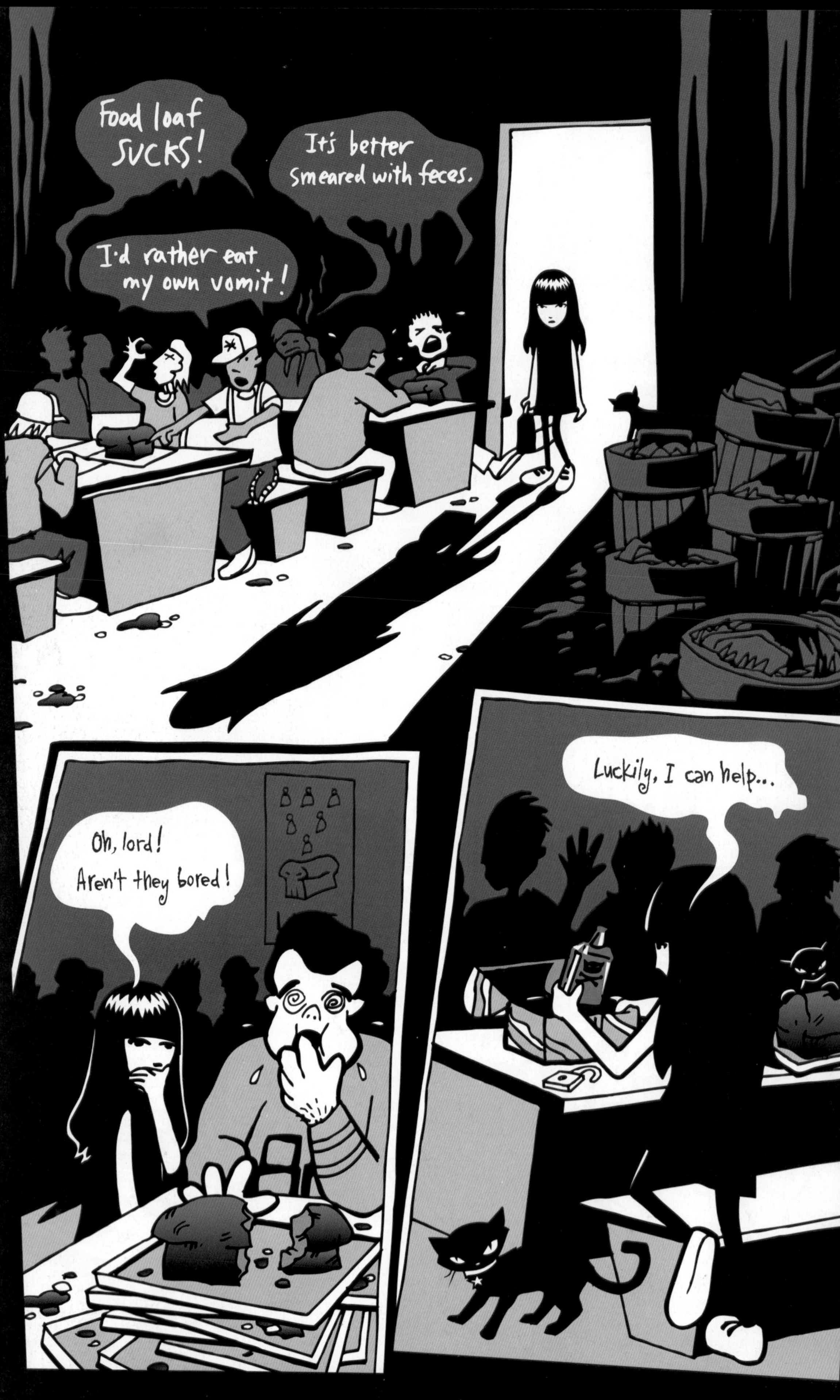
Food loaf SUCKS!
It's better smeared with feces.
I'd rather eat my own vomit!
Oh, lord! Aren't they bored!
Luckily, I can help...

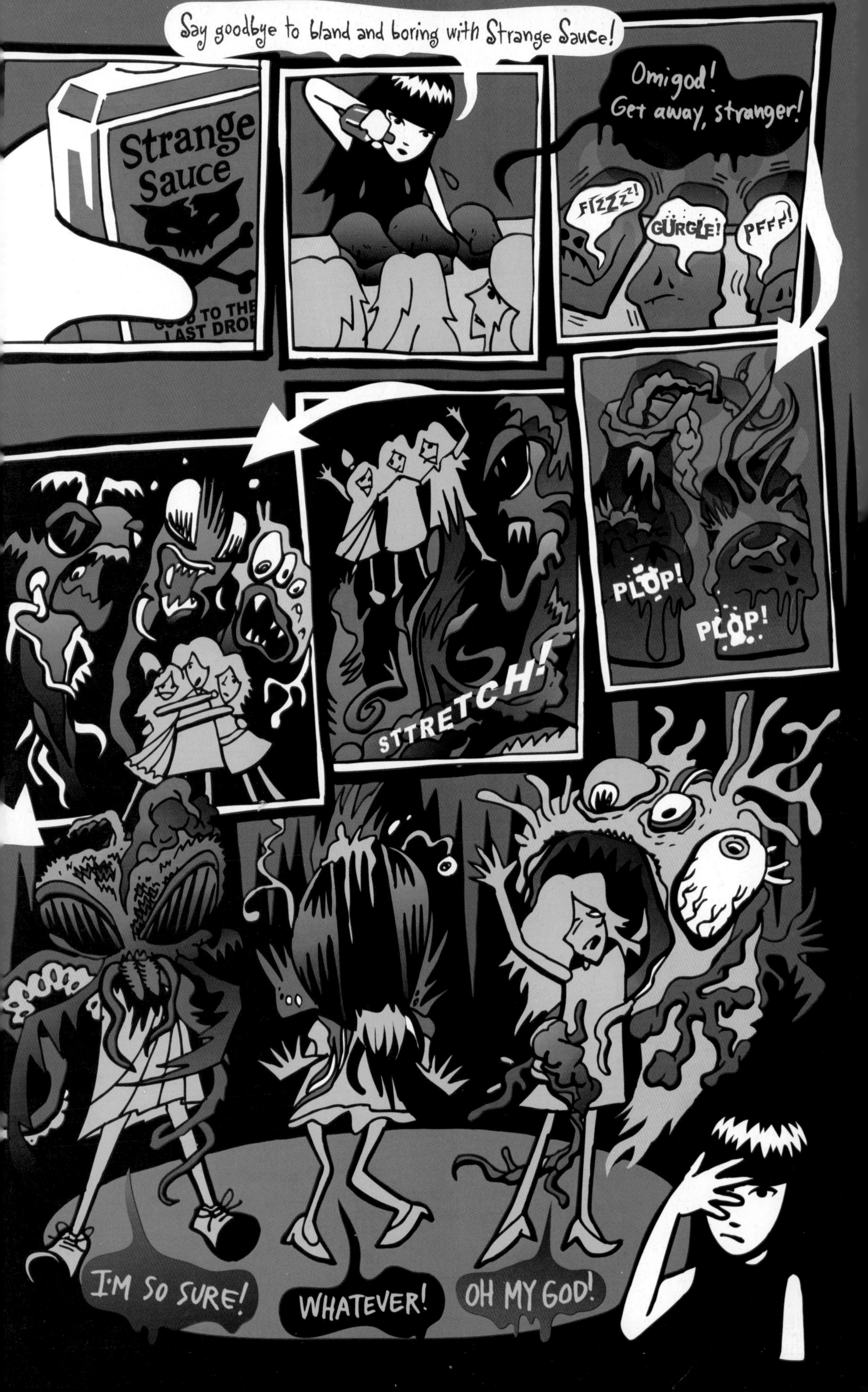
Say goodbye to bland and boring with Strange Sauce!
Strange Sauce
GOOD TO THE LAST DROP
Omigod! Get away, stranger!
FIZZZ!
GURGLE!
PFFF!
PLOP!
PLOP!
STTRETCH!
I'M SO SURE!
WHATEVER!
OH MY GOD!

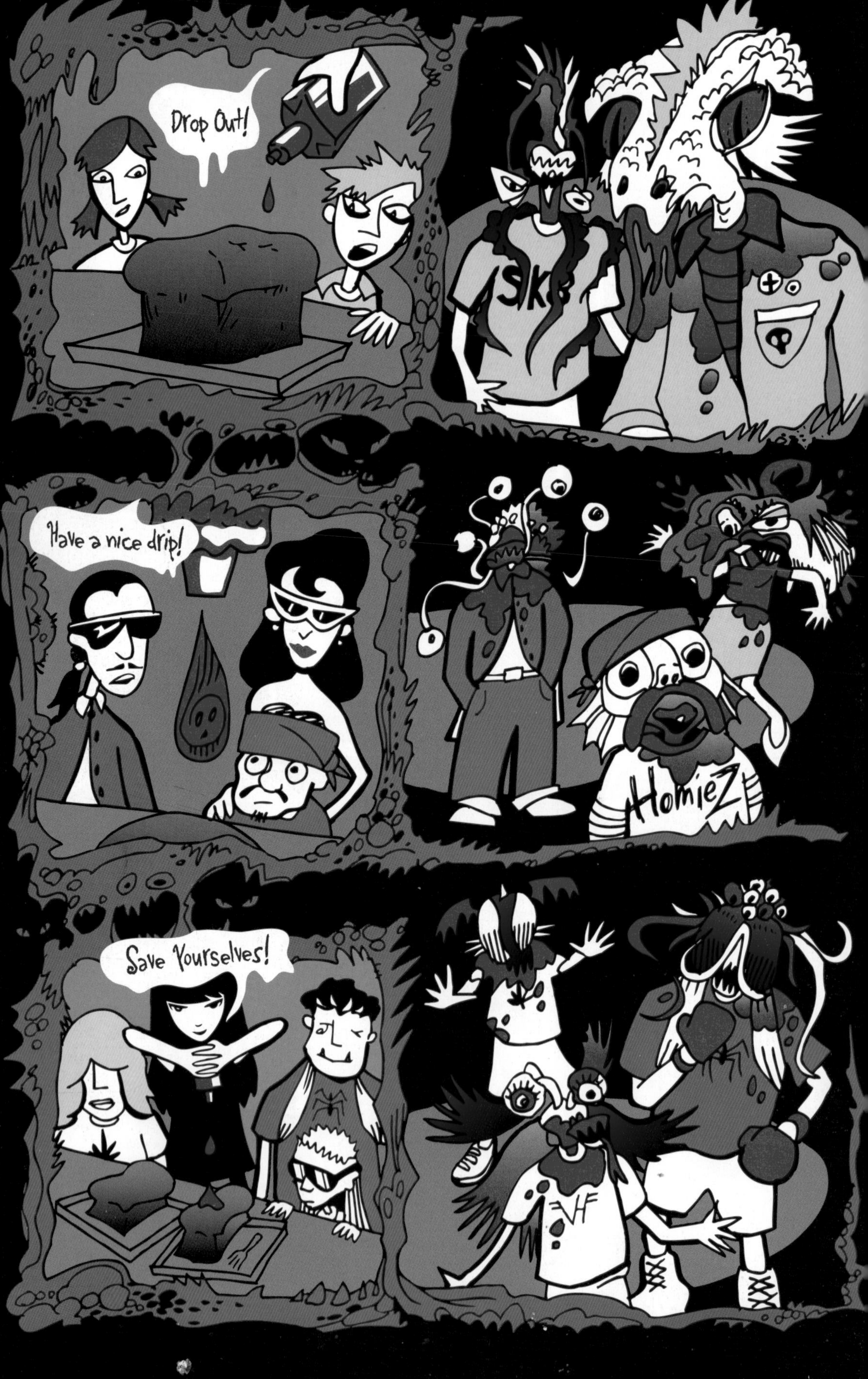
Drop Out!
SK8
Have a nice drip!
HomieZ
Save Yourselves!
VH

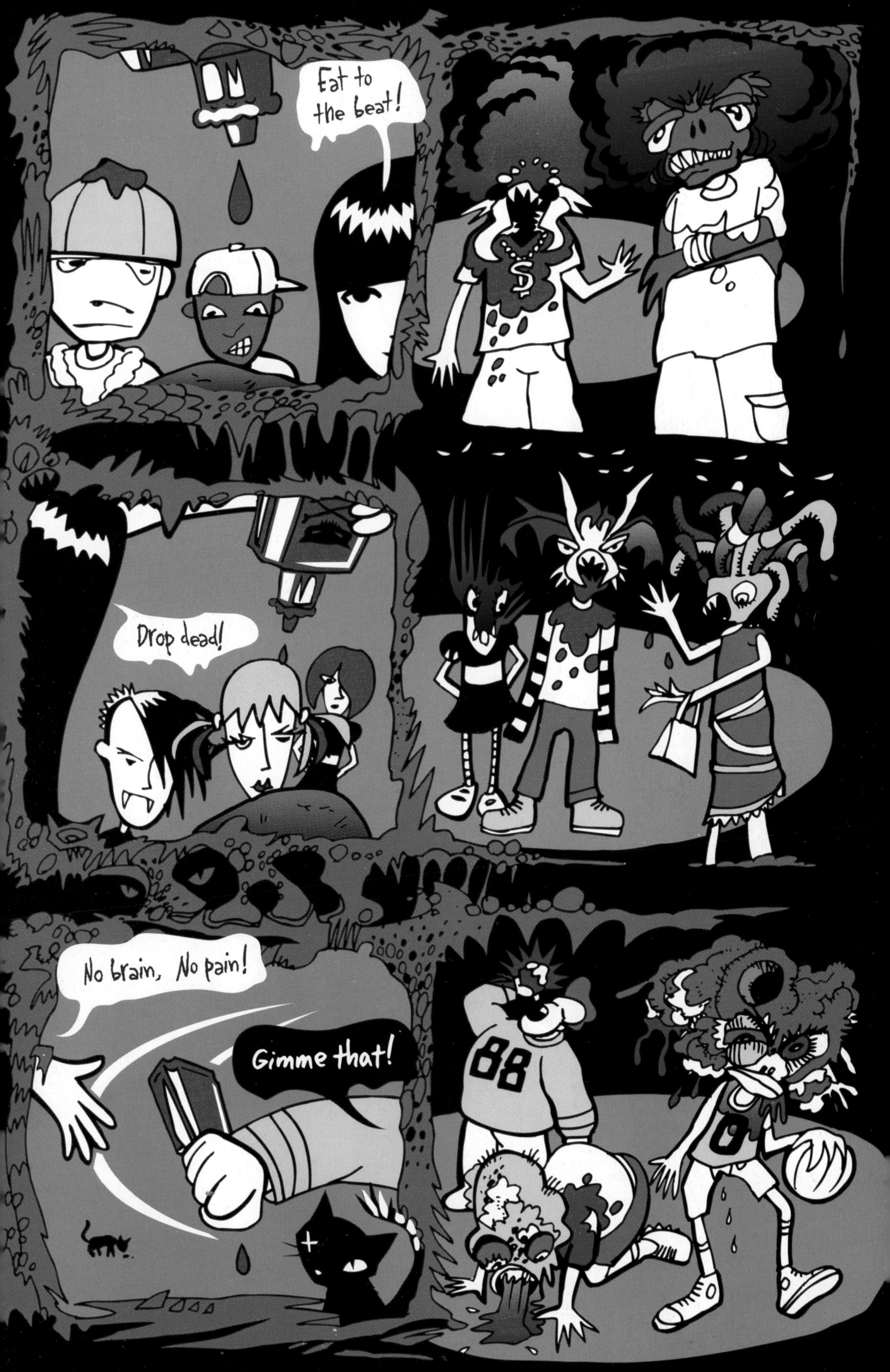
Eat to the beat!
Drop dead!
No brain, No pain!
Gimme that!

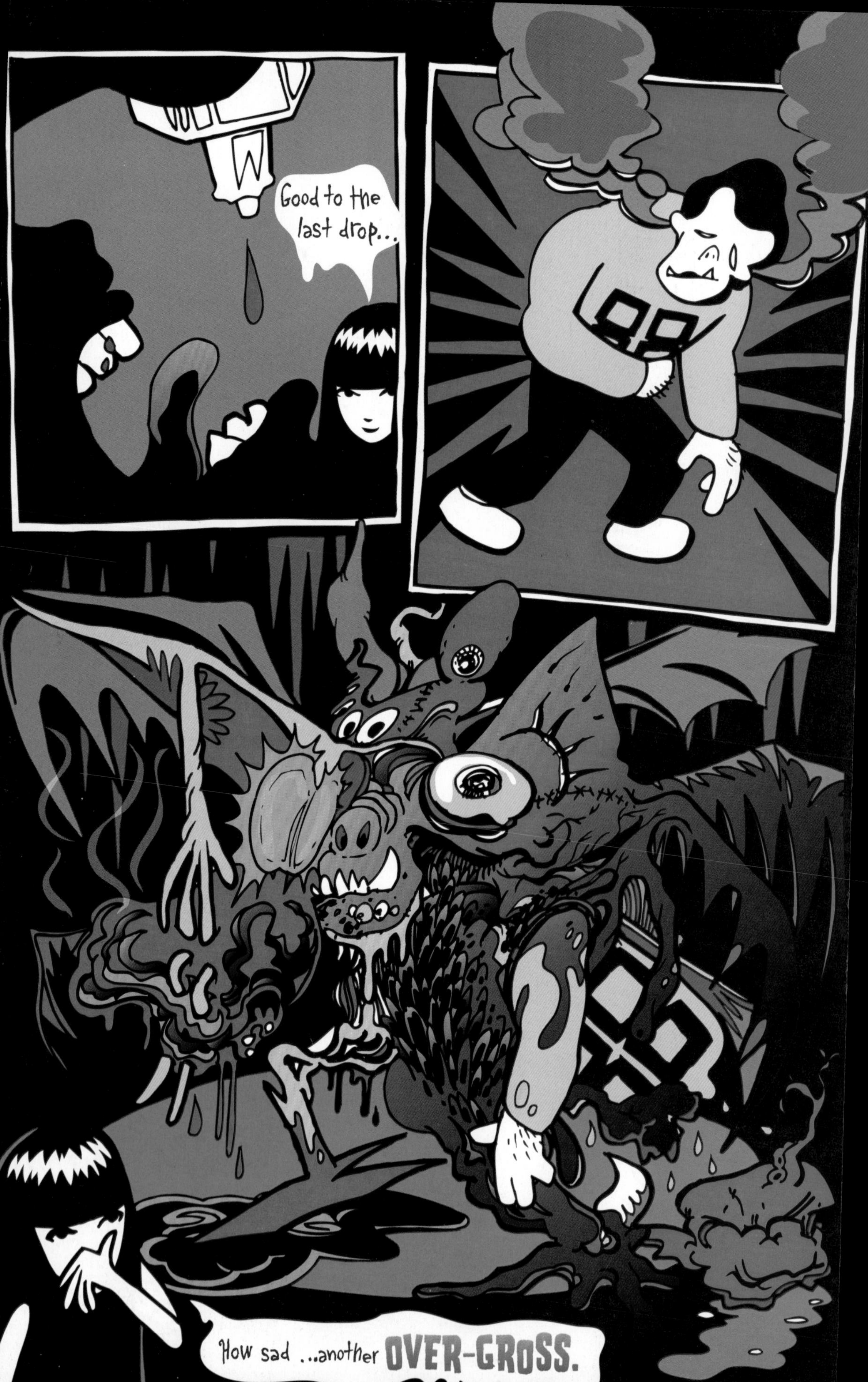
Good to the last drop...
How sad ...another OVER-GROSS.

 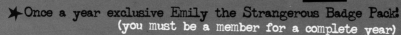

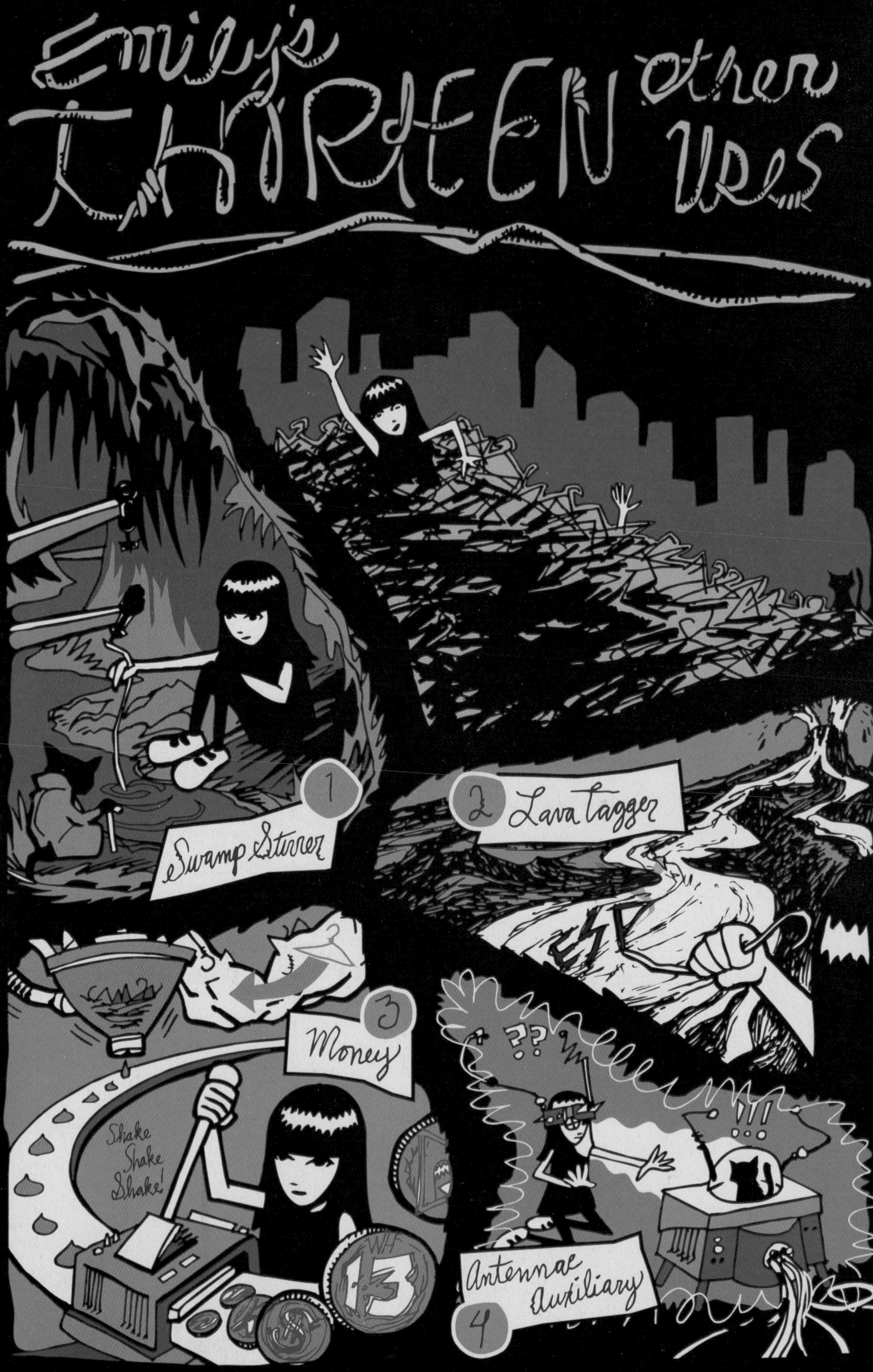
Emily's THIRTEEN other Uses
1
Swamp Stirrer
2 Lava Tagger
3
Money
Shake Shake Shake!
??
!!!
Antennae Auxiliary
4
13

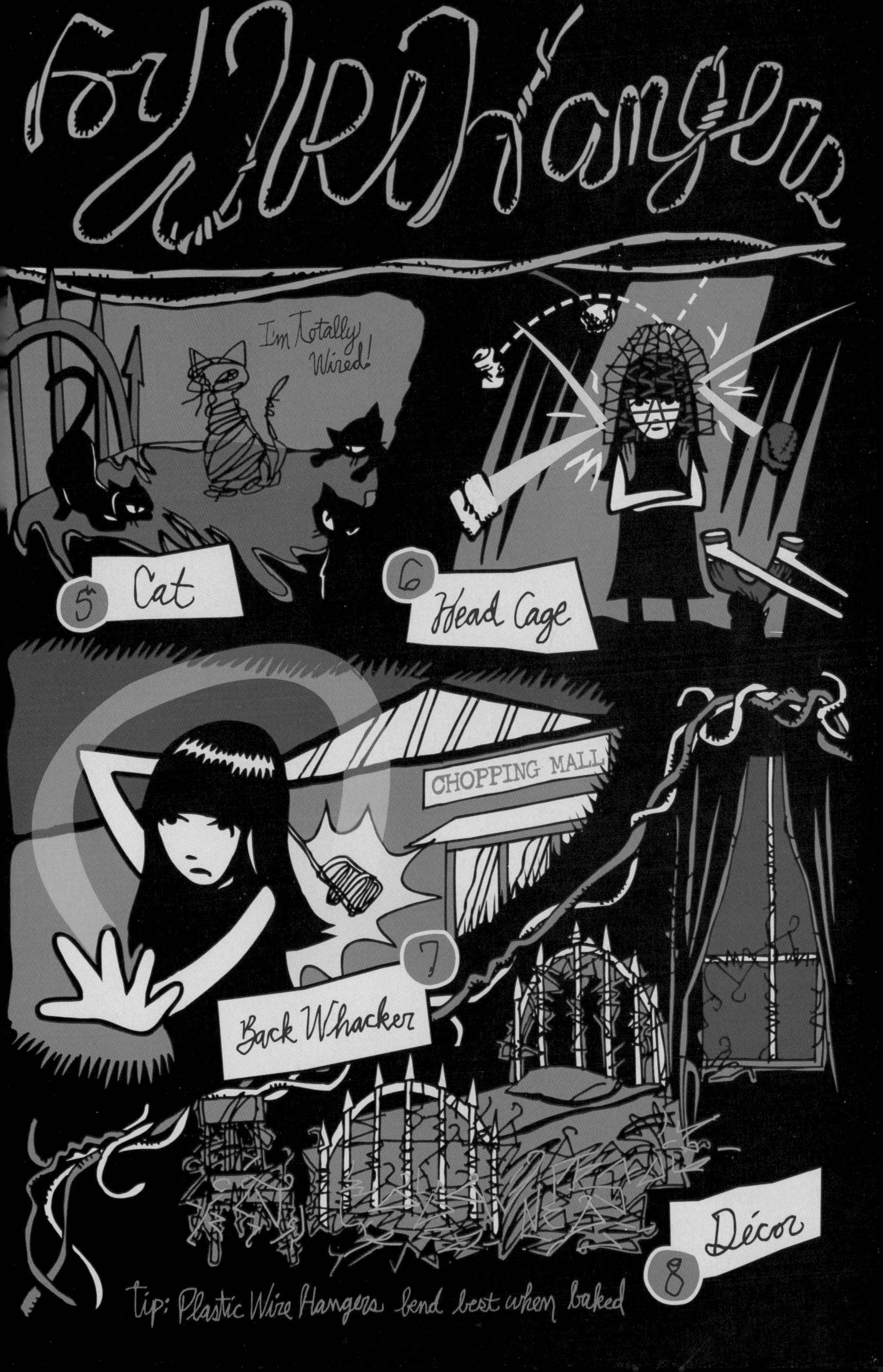
by Wire Hanger
I'm Totally Wired!
5 Cat
6 Head Cage
CHOPPING MALL
7 Back Whacker
8 Décor
tip: Plastic Wire Hangers bend best when baked

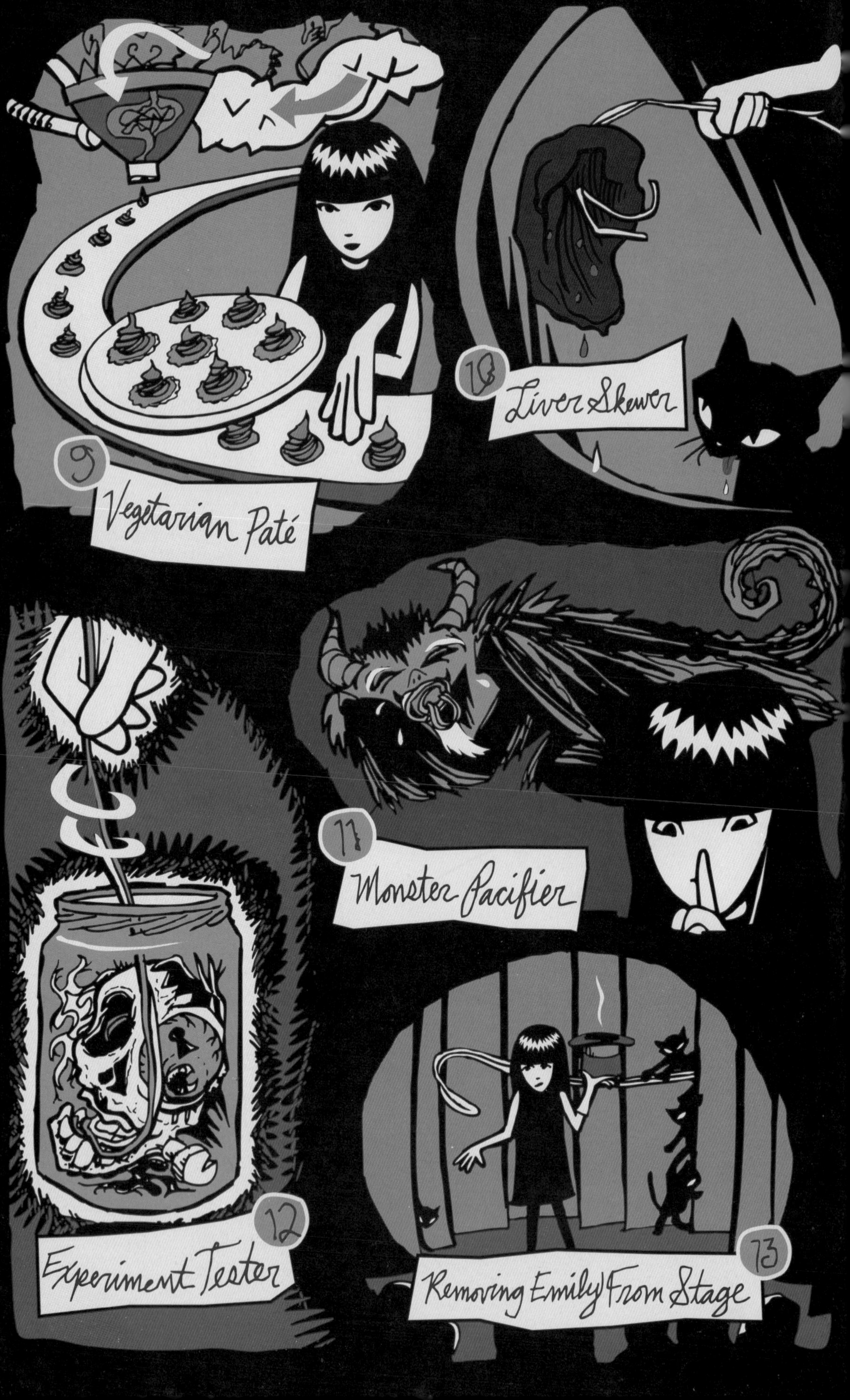
9
Vegetarian Paté
10
Liver Skewer
11
Monster Pacifier
12
Experiment Tester
13
Removing Emily From Stage

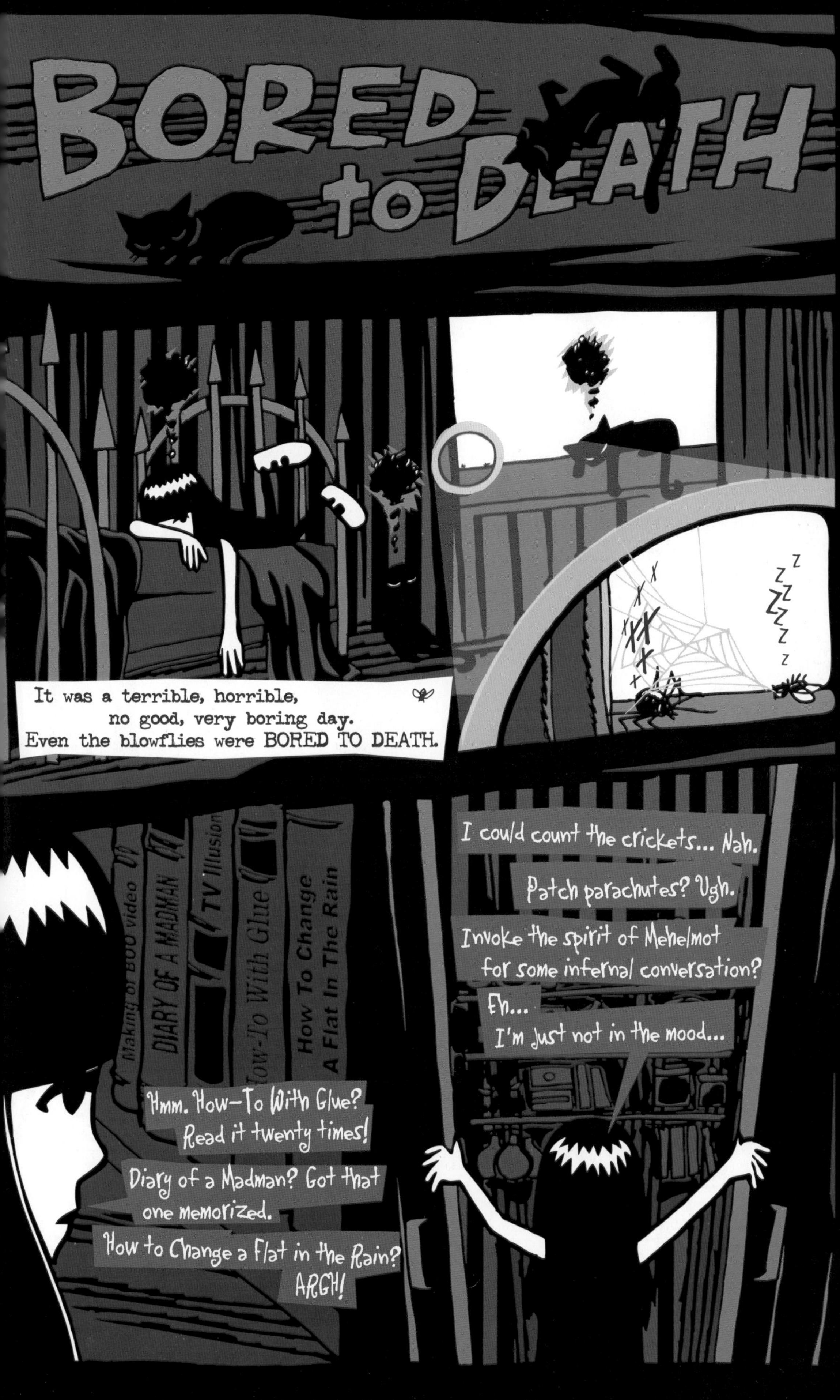
BORED to DEATH
It was a terrible, horrible, no good, very boring day. Even the blowflies were BORED TO DEATH.
Z Z Z Z Z Z Z
Making of BOO video
DIARY OF A MADMAN
TV Illusion
How-To With Glue
How To Change A Flat In The Rain
Hmm. How-To With Glue? Read it twenty times!
Diary of a Madman? Got that one memorized.
How to Change a Flat in the Rain? ARGH!
I could count the crickets... Nah.
Patch parachutes? Ugh.
Invoke the spirit of Mehelmot for some infernal conversation?
Eh... I'm just not in the mood...

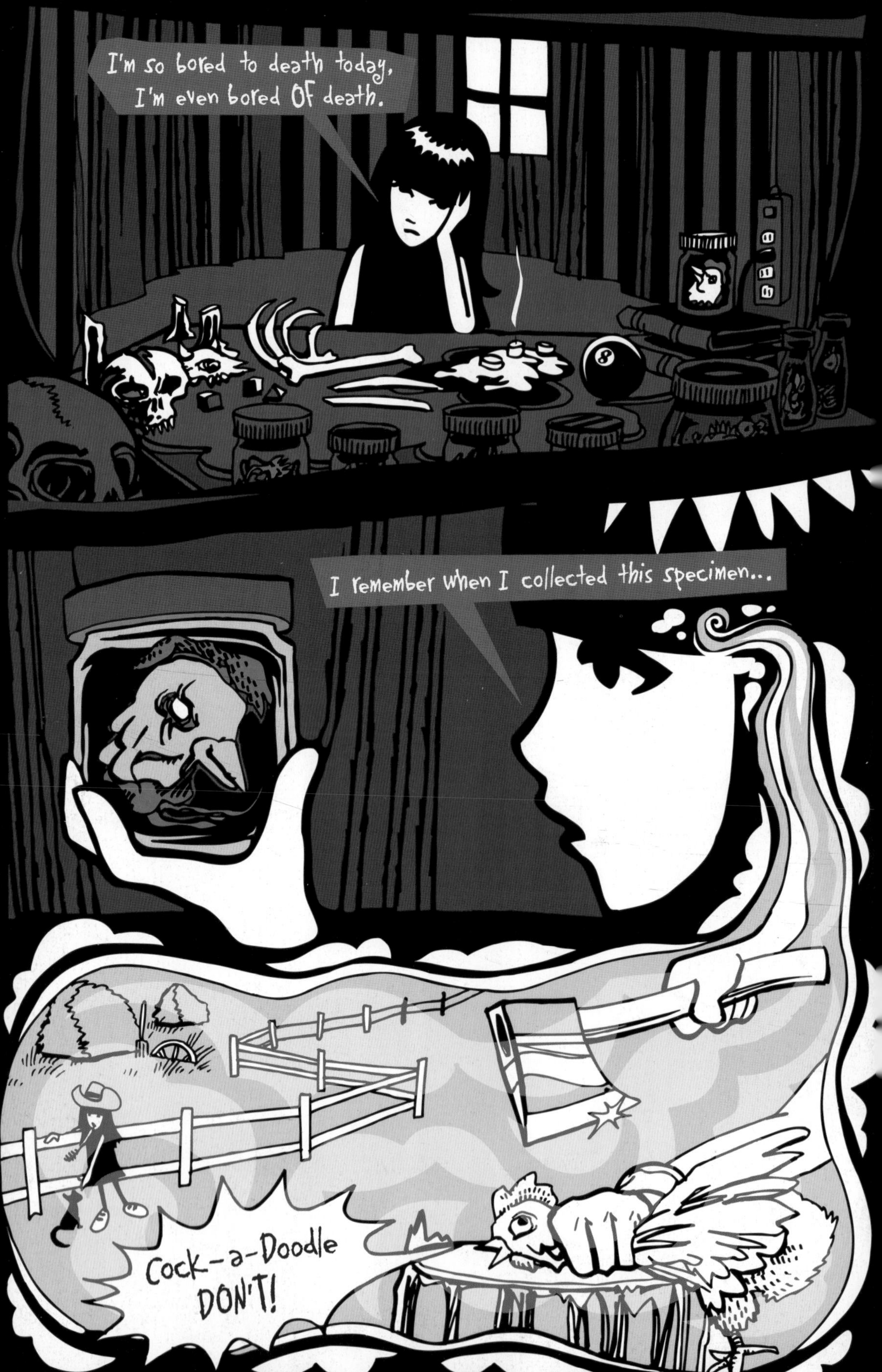

I'm so bored to death today, I'm even bored OF death.
I remember when I collected this specimen...
Cock-a-Doodle DON'T!

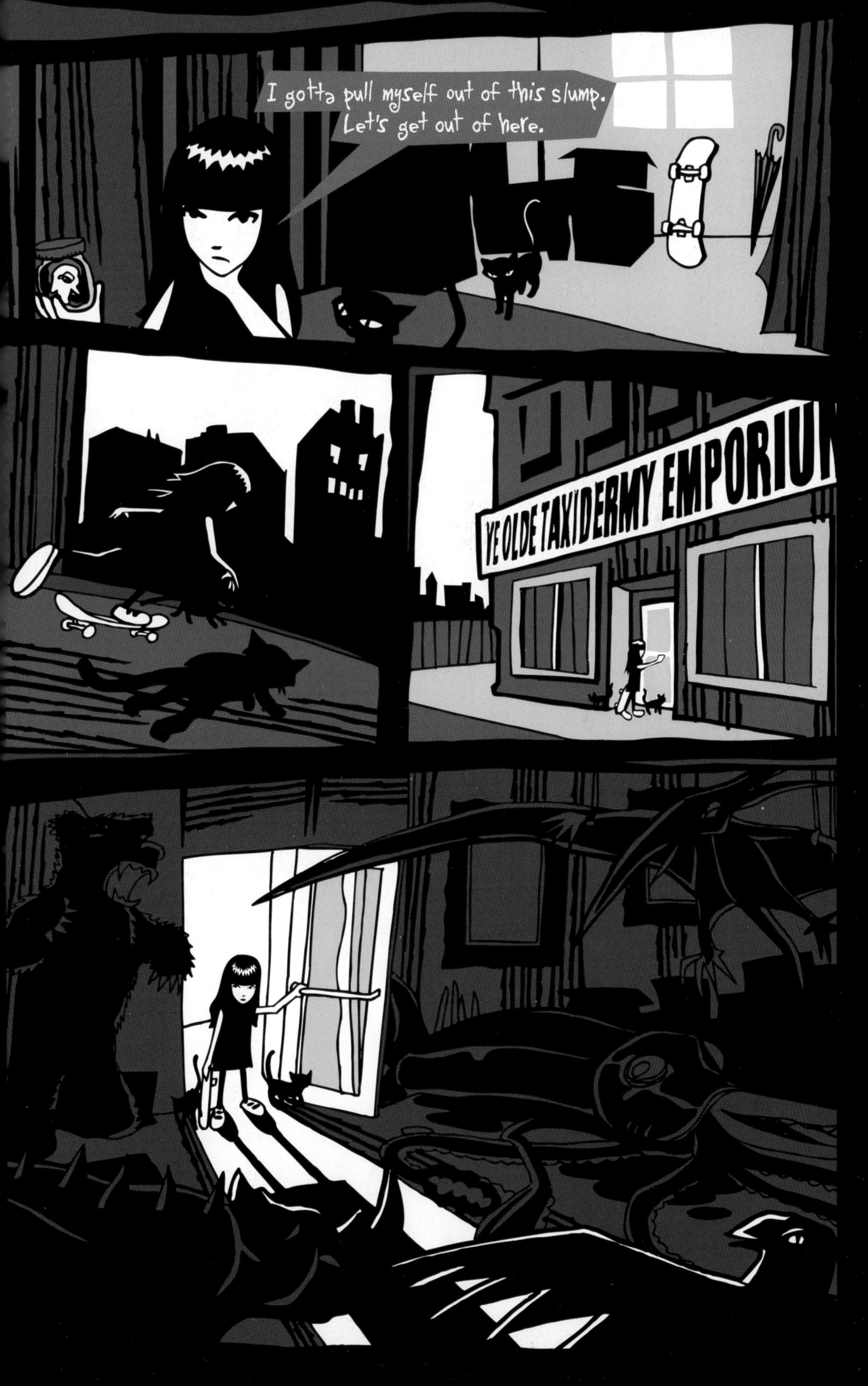
I gotta pull myself out of this slump.
Let's get out of here.
YE OLDE TAXIDERMY EMPORIU

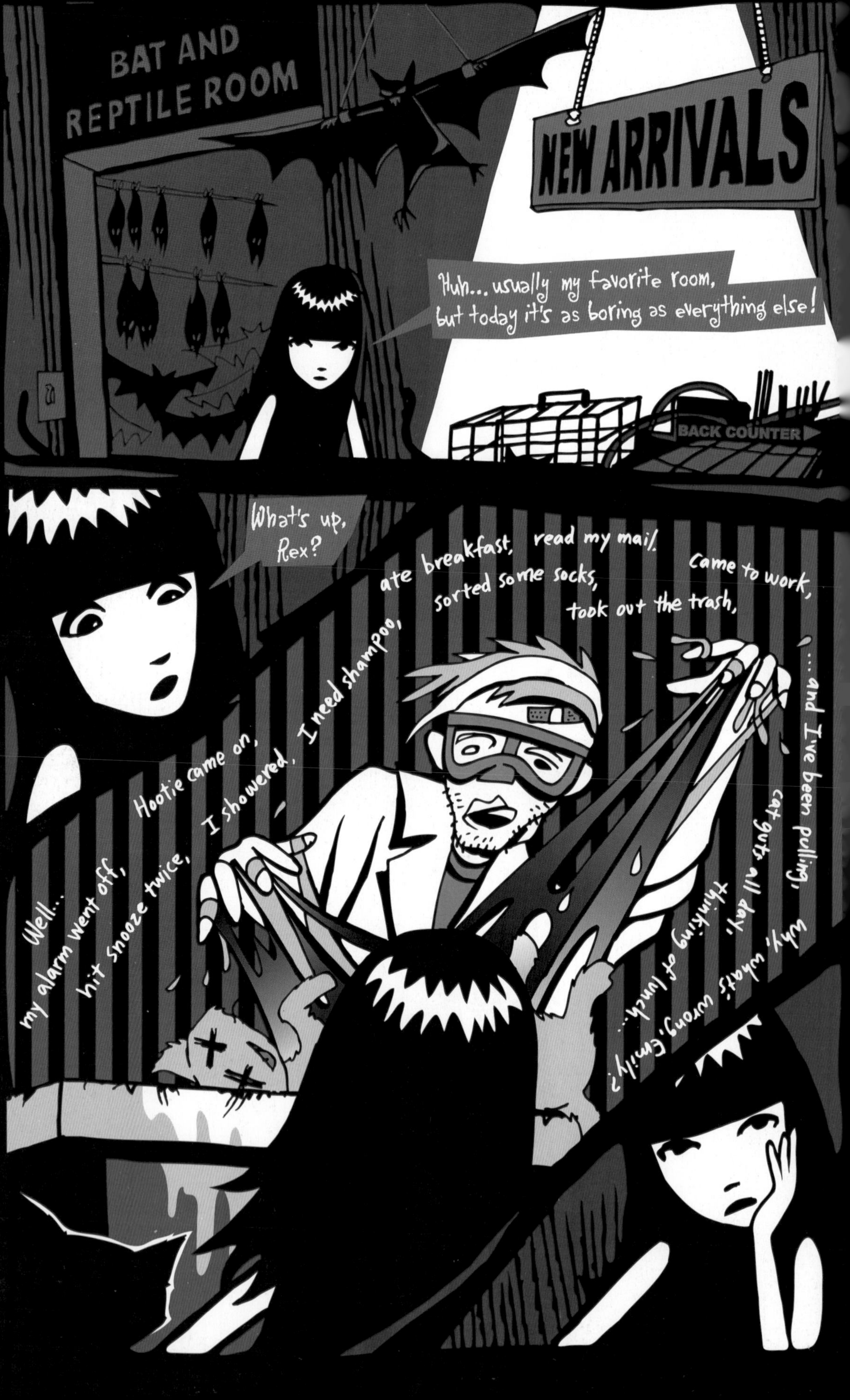
BAT AND REPTILE ROOM
NEW ARRIVALS
Huh... usually my favorite room, but today it's as boring as everything else!
BACK COUNTER
What's up, Rex?
Well... my alarm went off, hit snooze twice, Hootie came on, I showered, I need shampoo, ate breakfast, sorted some socks, read my mail, took out the trash, came to work,
...and I've been pulling cat guts all day, thinking of lunch...
why, what's wrong, Emily?

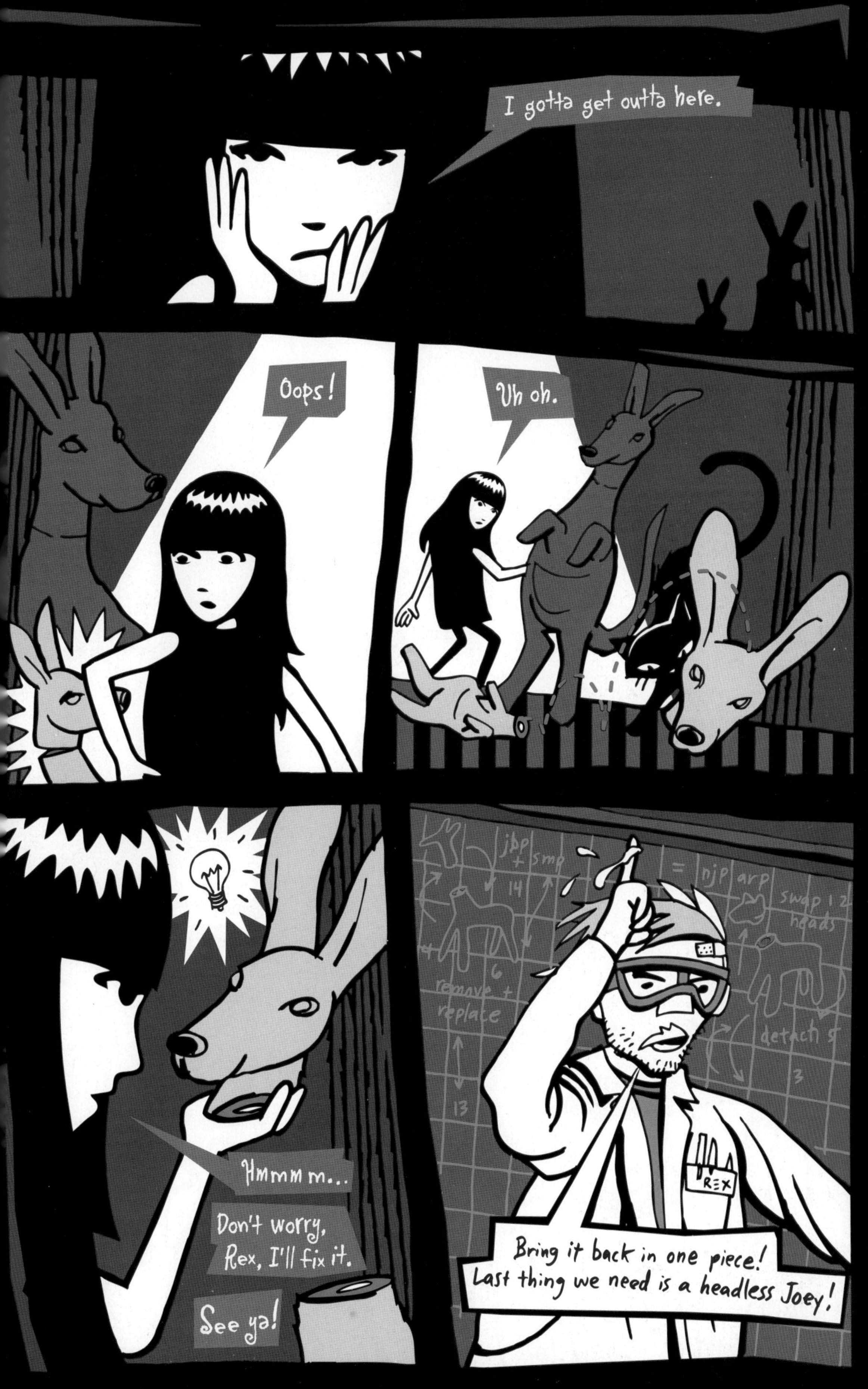
I gotta get outta here.
Oops!
Uh oh.
Hmmm m...
Don't worry, Rex, I'll fix it.
See ya!
Bring it back in one piece! Last thing we need is a headless Joey!
REX

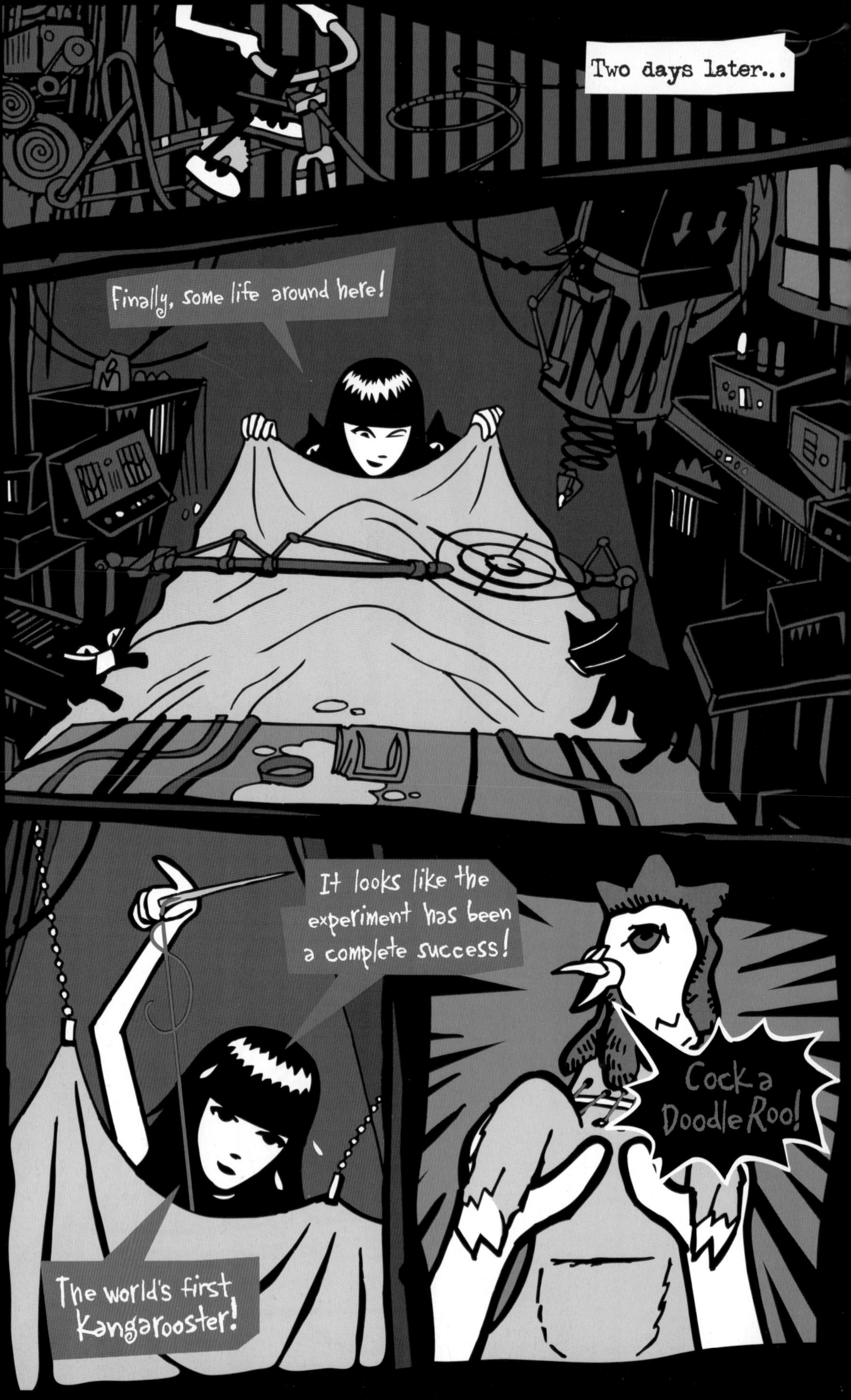

Two days later...
Finally, some life around here!
It looks like the experiment has been a complete success!
The world's first Kangarooster!
Cock a Doodle Roo!

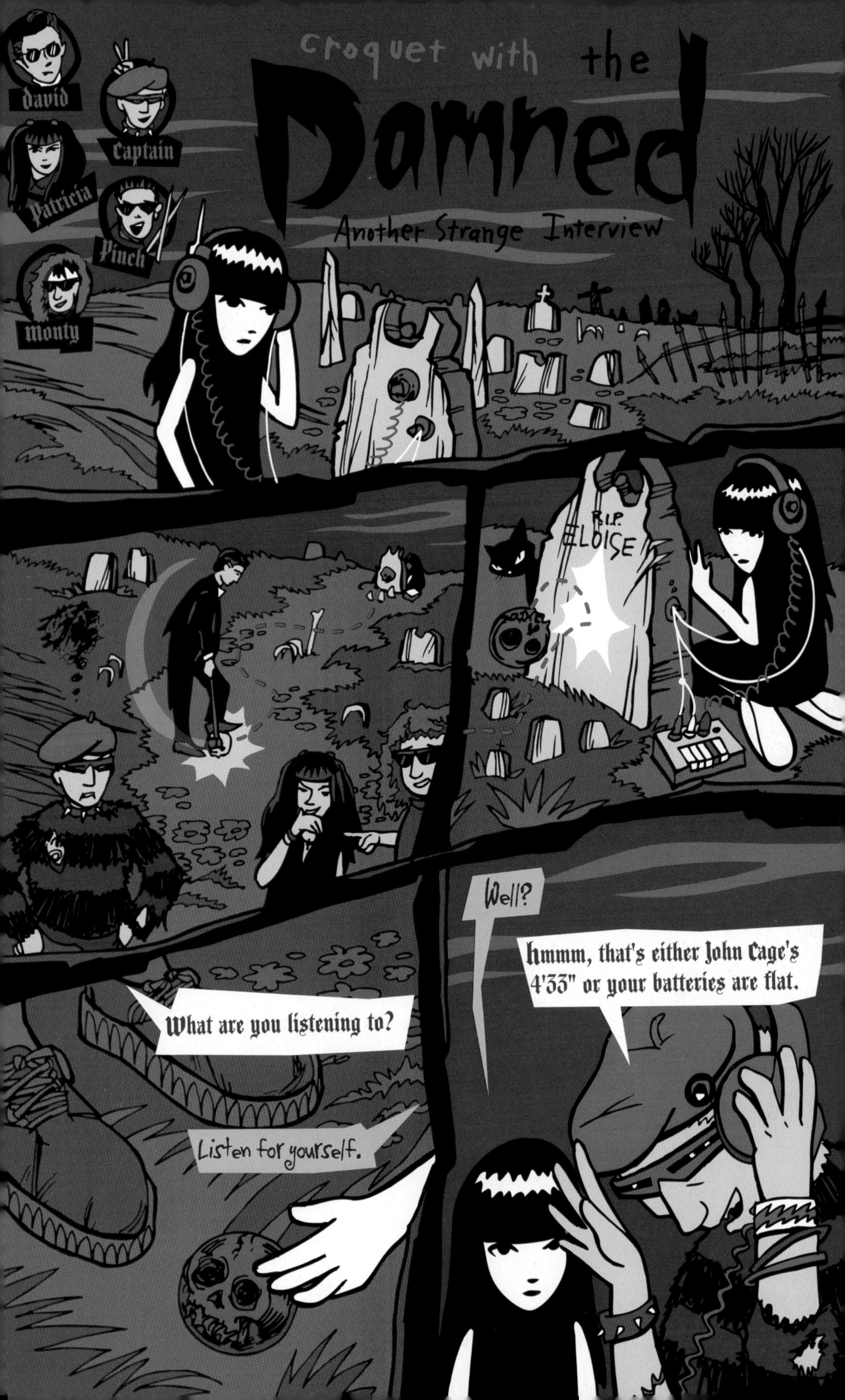

croquet with the Damned
Another Strange Interview
david
captain
Patricia
Pinch
monty
R.I.P. ELOISE
What are you listening to?
Listen for yourself.
Well?
hmmm, that's either John Cage's 4'33" or your batteries are flat.

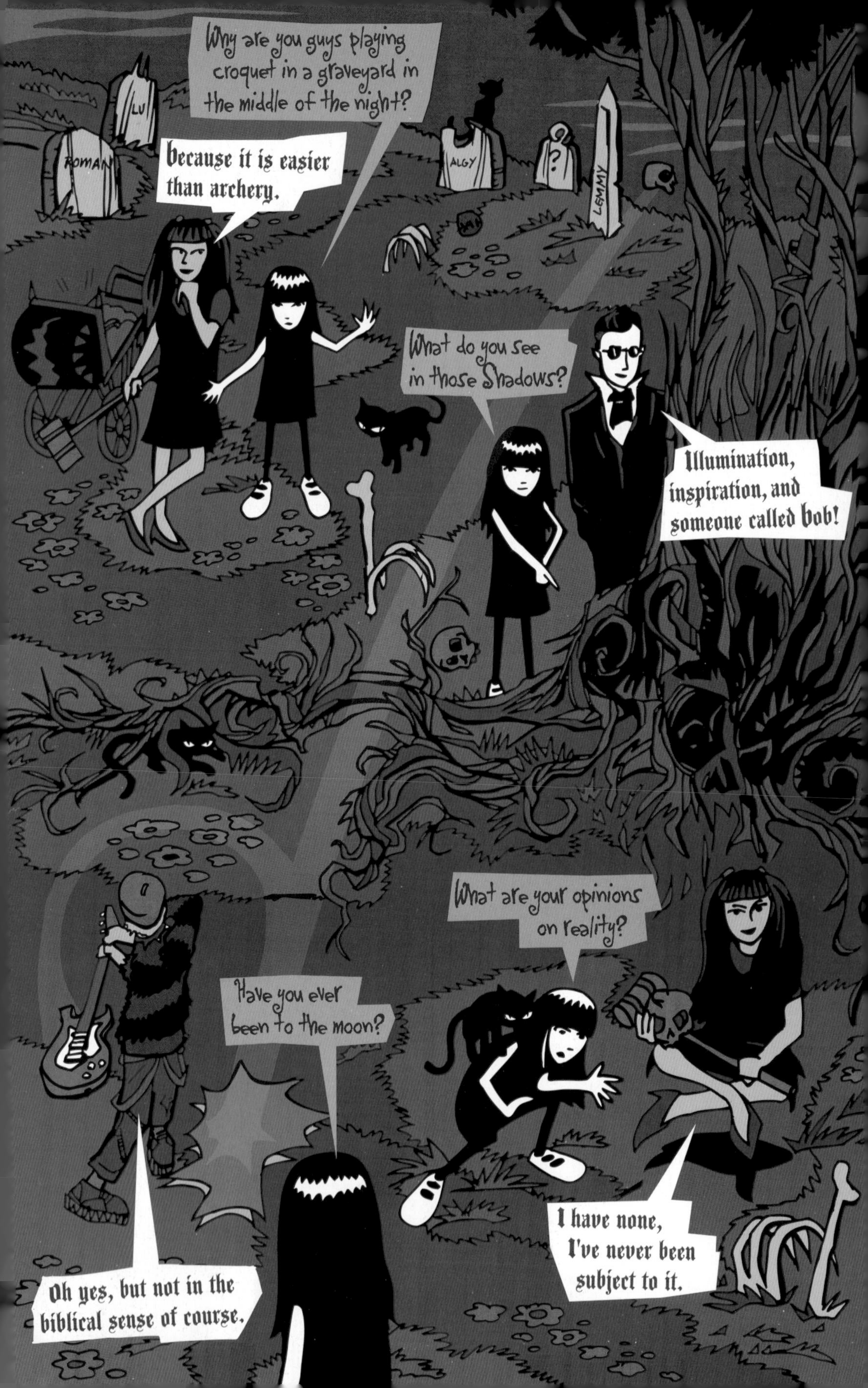

LU
ROMAN
ALGY
?
LEMMY
Why are you guys playing croquet in a graveyard in the middle of the night?
because it is easier than archery.
What do you see in those Shadows?
Illumination, inspiration, and someone called bob!
What are your opinions on reality?
I have none, I've never been subject to it.
Have you ever been to the moon?
Oh yes, but not in the biblical sense of course.

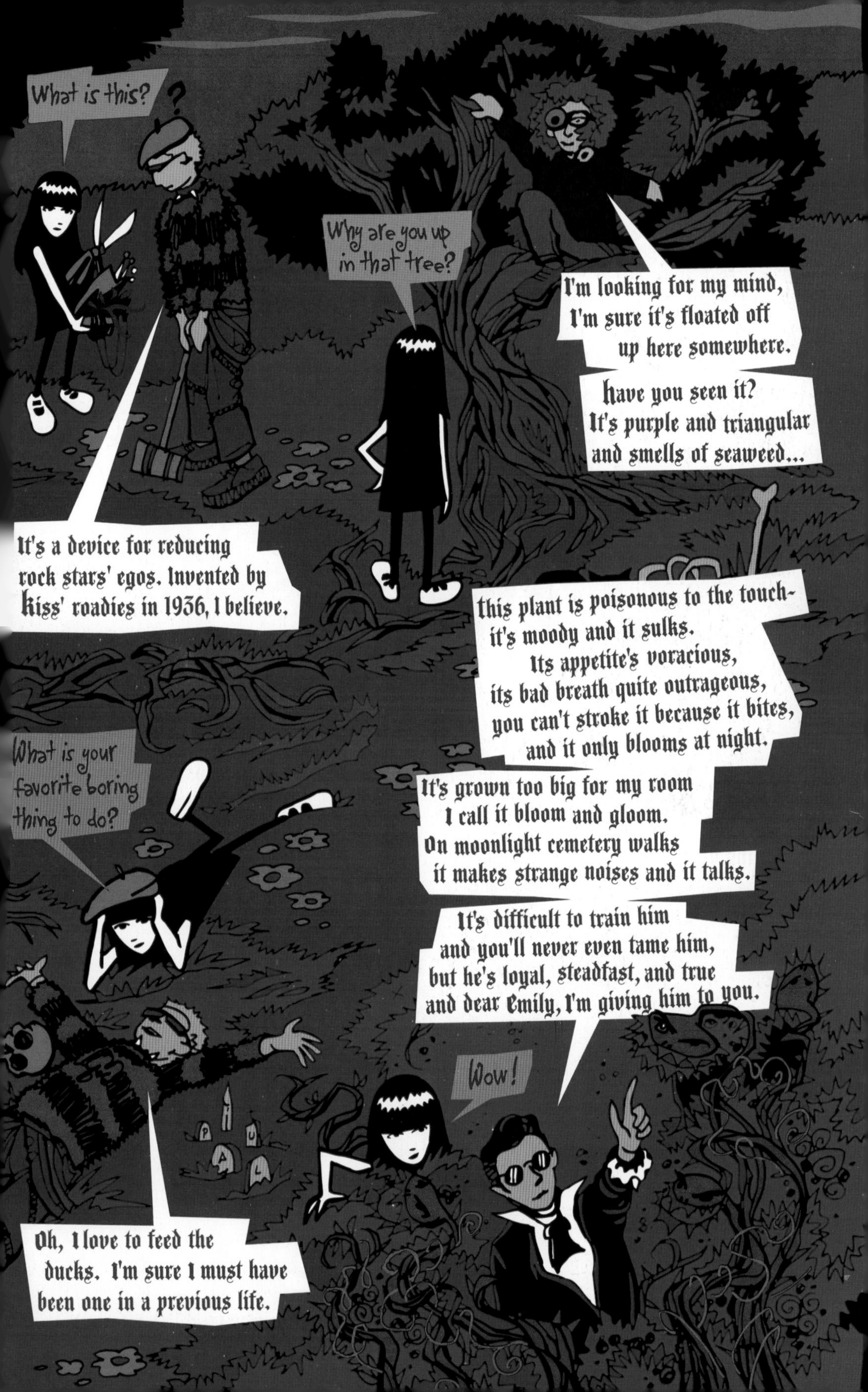
What is this?
It's a device for reducing rock stars' egos. Invented by Kiss' roadies in 1936, I believe.
Why are you up in that tree?
I'm looking for my mind, I'm sure it's floated off up here somewhere.
Have you seen it? It's purple and triangular and smells of seaweed...
What is your favorite boring thing to do?
Oh, I love to feed the ducks. I'm sure I must have been one in a previous life.
this plant is poisonous to the touch-
it's moody and it sulks.
Its appetite's voracious,
its bad breath quite outrageous,
you can't stroke it because it bites,
and it only blooms at night.
It's grown too big for my room
I call it bloom and gloom.
On moonlight cemetery walks
it makes strange noises and it talks.
It's difficult to train him
and you'll never even tame him,
but he's loyal, steadfast, and true
and dear Emily, I'm giving him to you.
Wow!
PAUL

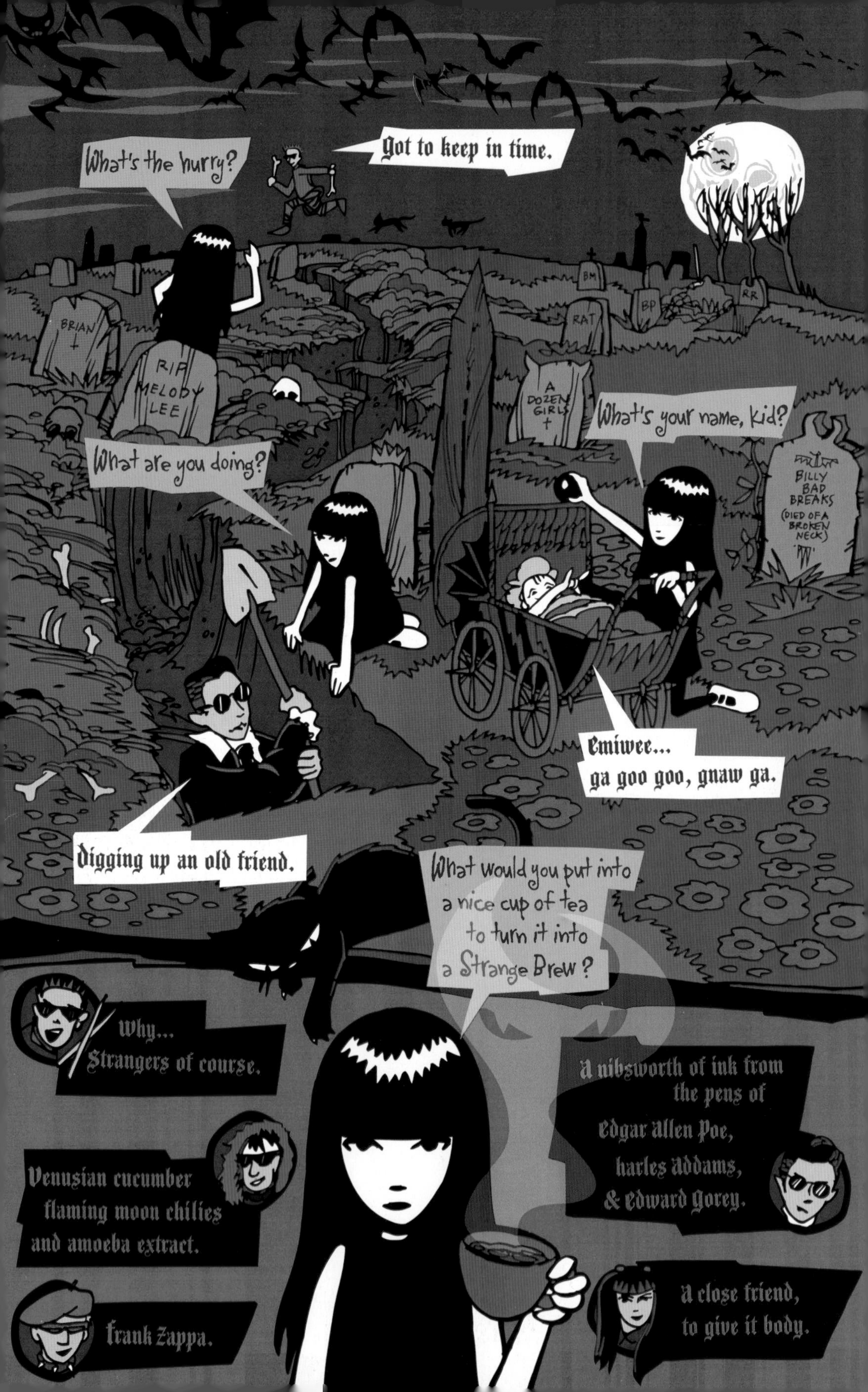
What's the hurry?
Got to keep in time.
BRIAN
RIP MELODY LEE
BM
RAT
BP
RR
A DOZEN GIRLS
What are you doing?
Digging up an old friend.
BILLY BAD BREAKS (DIED OF A BROKEN NECK)
What's your name, kid?
Emiwee... ga goo goo, gnaw ga.
What would you put into a nice cup of tea to turn it into a Strange Brew?
Why... Strangers of course.
Venusian cucumber flaming moon chilies and amoeba extract.
Frank Zappa.
A nibsworth of ink from the pens of Edgar Allen Poe, harles Addams, & Edward Gorey.
A close friend, to give it body.

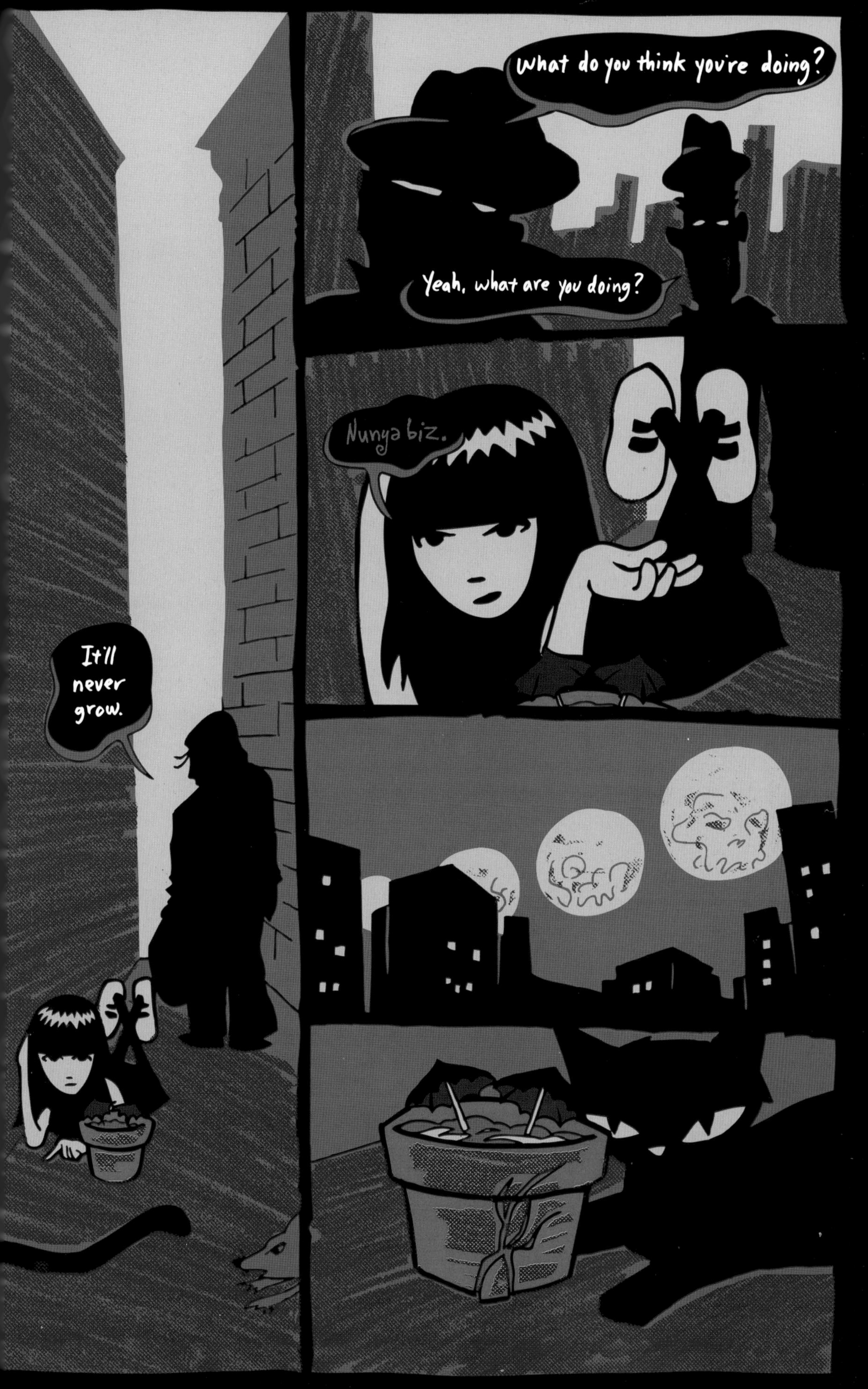
It'll never grow.
What do you think you're doing?
Yeah, what are you doing?
Nunya biz.

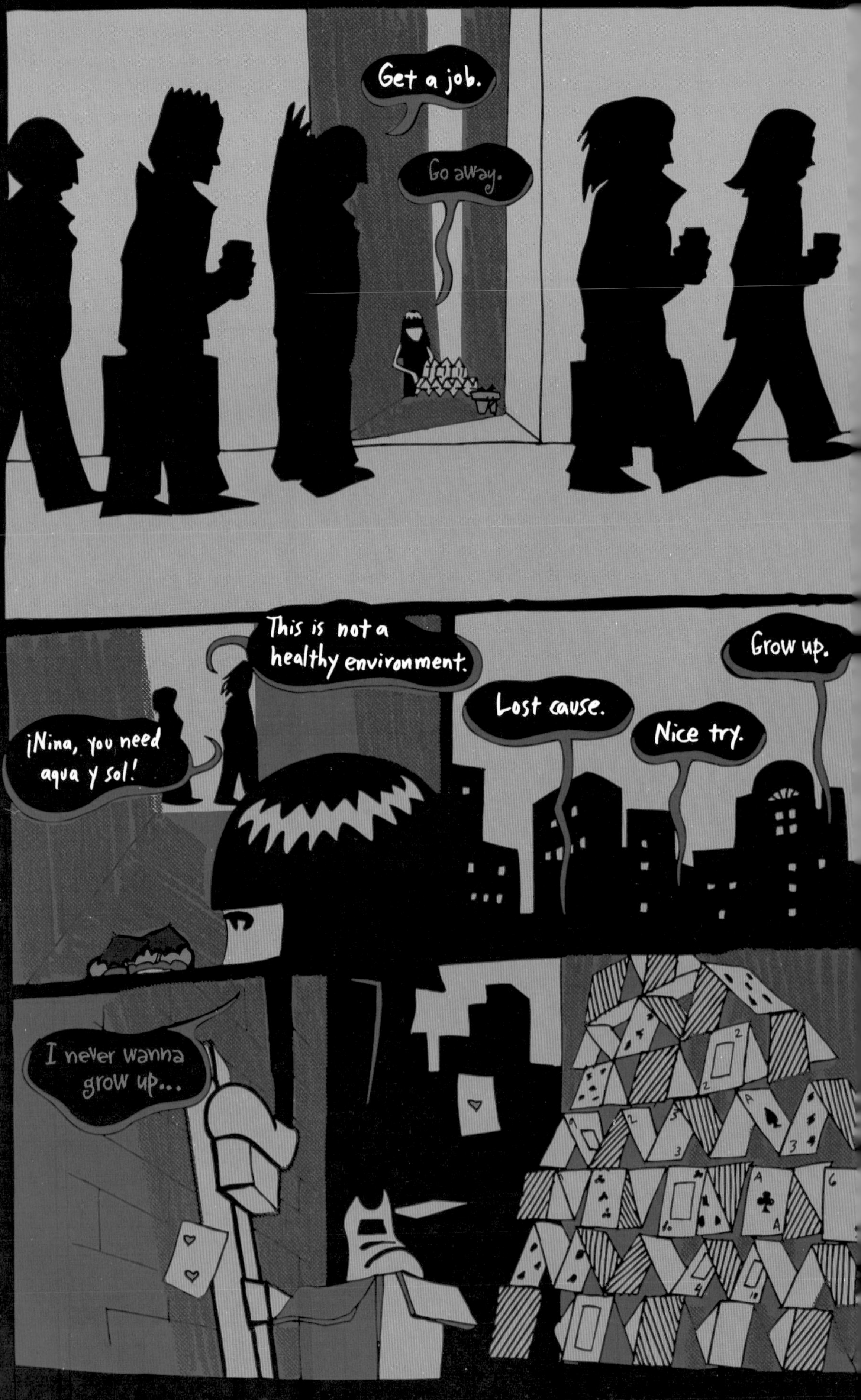
Get a job.
Go away.
This is not a healthy environment.
Grow up.
Lost cause.
Nice try.
¡Nina, you need aqua y sol!
I never wanna grow up...

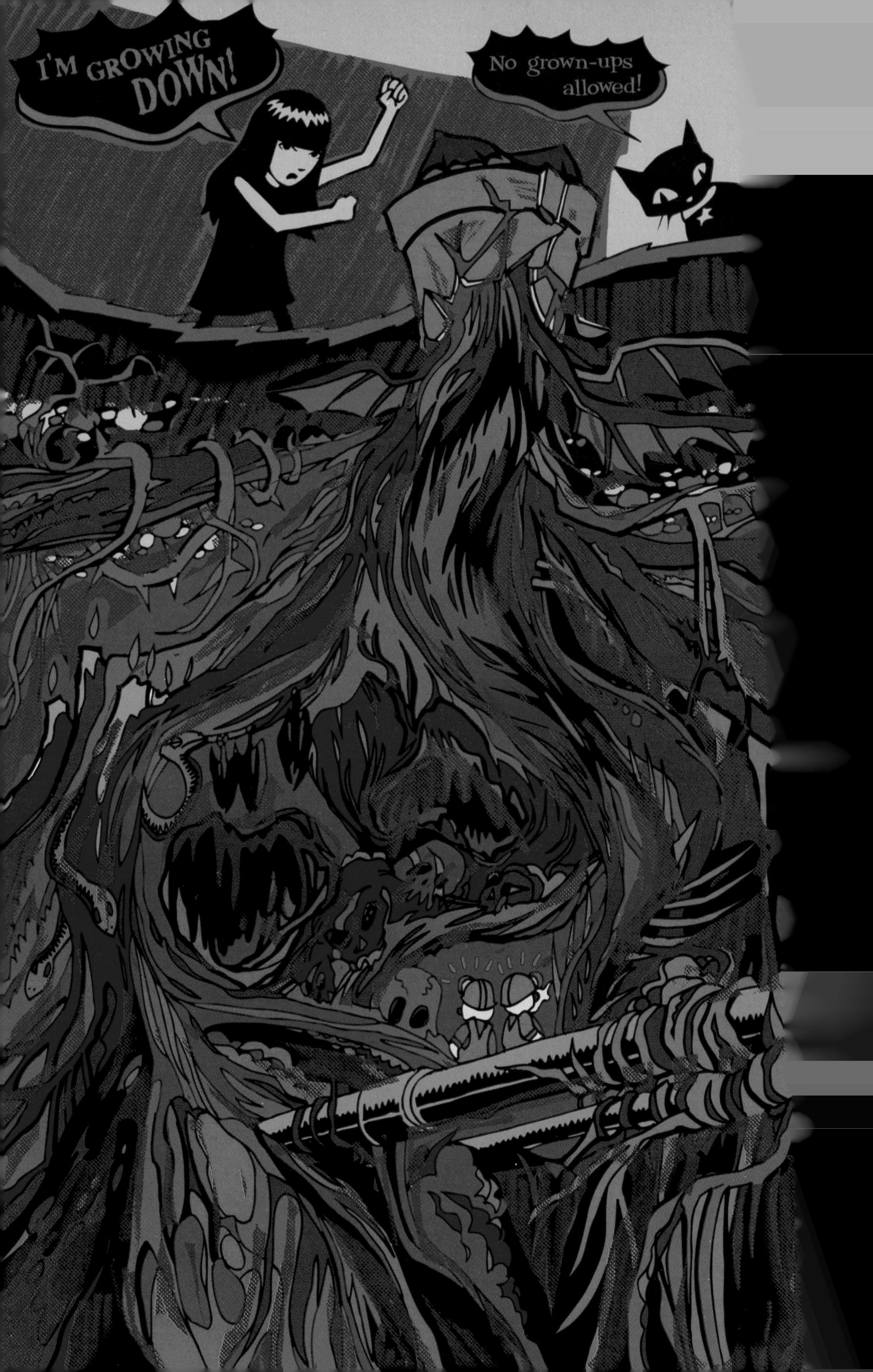
I'M GROWING DOWN!
No grown-ups allowed!

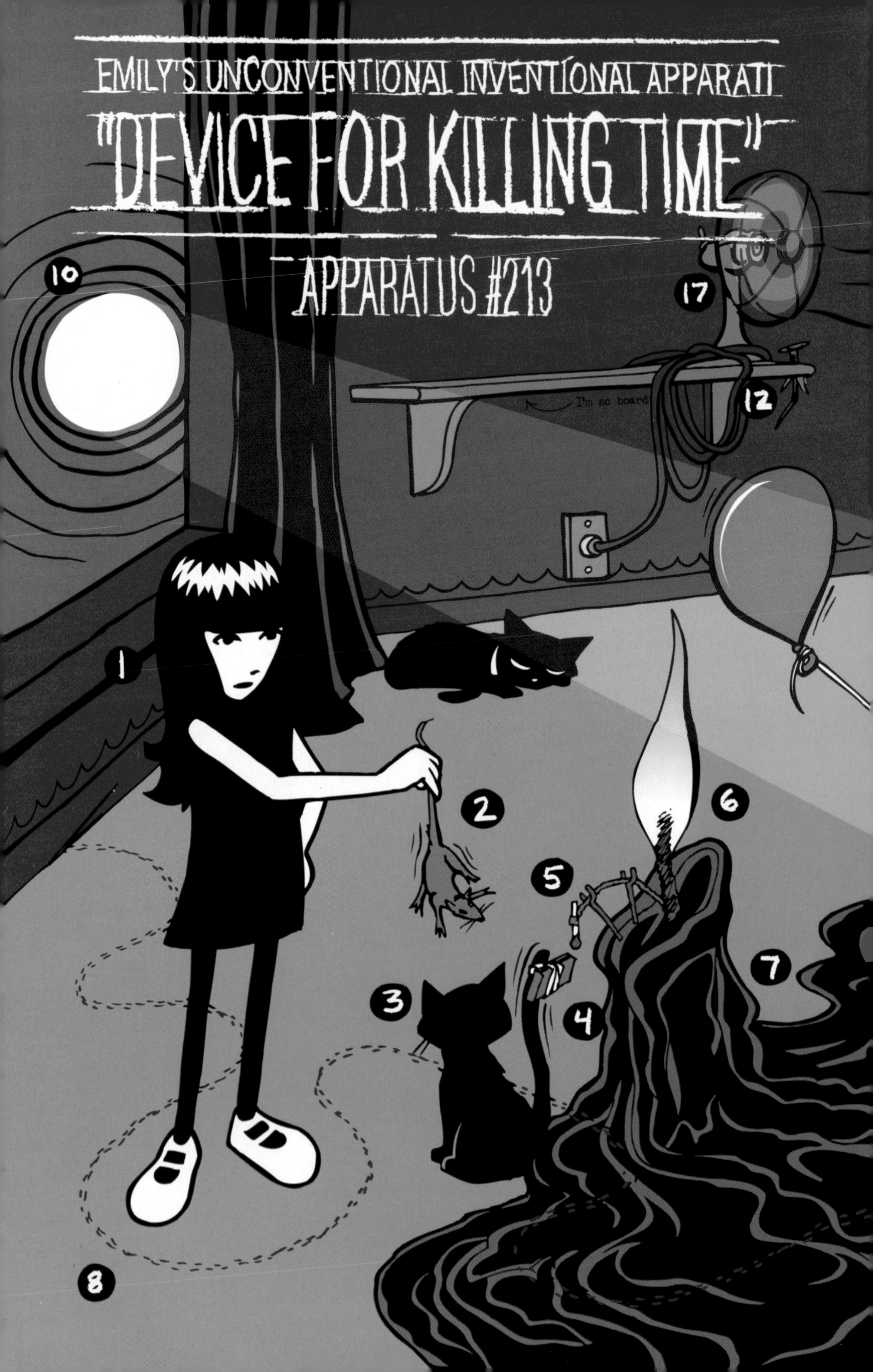

EMILY'S UNCONVENTIONAL INVENTIONAL APPARATI
"DEVICE FOR KILLING TIME"
APPARATUS #213
10
17
I'm so board
12
1
2
6
5
7
3
4
8

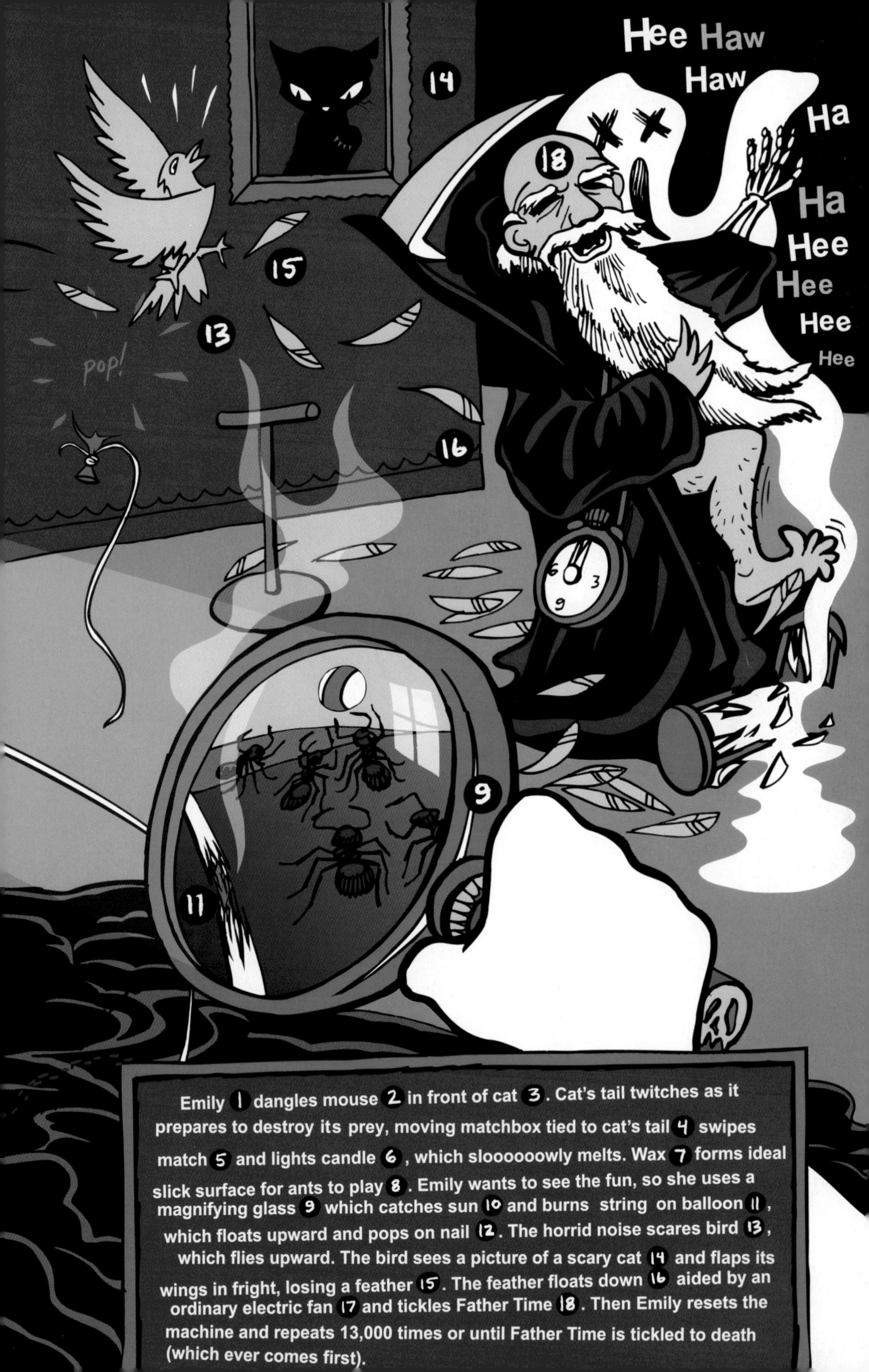
Hee Haw
Haw
Ha
Ha
Hee
Hee
Hee
Hee
14
18
15
13
pop!
16
9
11

Emily (1) dangles mouse (2) in front of cat (3). Cat's tail twitches as it prepares to destroy its prey, moving matchbox tied to cat's tail (4) swipes match (5) and lights candle (6), which slooooowly melts. Wax (7) forms ideal slick surface for ants to play (8). Emily wants to see the fun, so she uses a magnifying glass (9) which catches sun (10) and burns string on balloon (11), which floats upward and pops on nail (12). The horrid noise scares bird (13), which flies upward. The bird sees a picture of a scary cat (14) and flaps its wings in fright, losing a feather (15). The feather floats down (16) aided by an ordinary electric fan (17) and tickles Father Time (18). Then Emily resets the machine and repeats 13,000 times or until Father Time is tickled to death (which ever comes first).

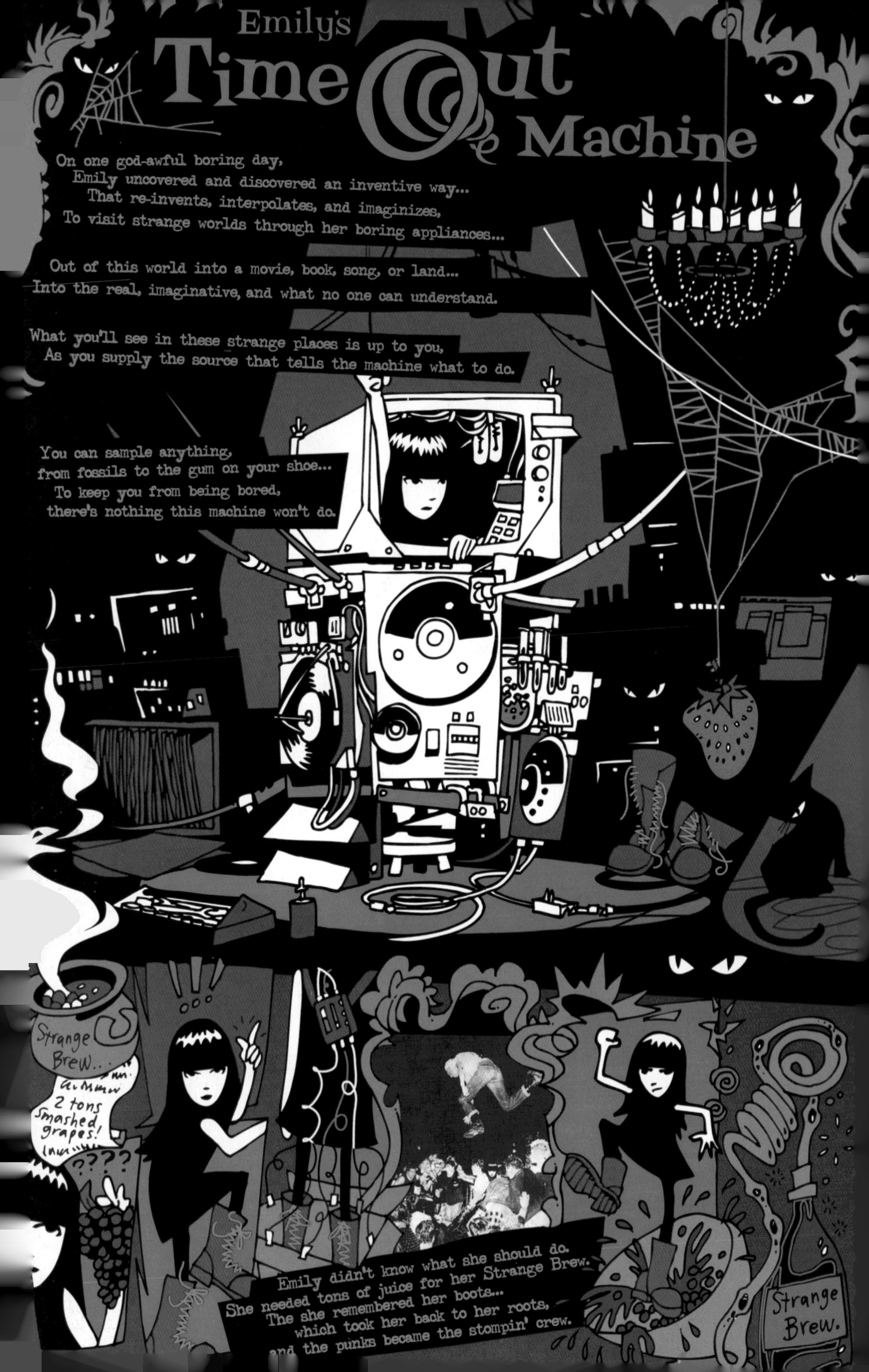
Emily's
Time Out Machine
On one god-awful boring day,
Emily uncovered and discovered an inventive way...
That re-invents, interpolates, and imaginizes,
To visit strange worlds through her boring appliances...
Out of this world into a movie, book, song, or land...
Into the real, imaginative, and what no one can understand.
What you'll see in these strange places is up to you,
As you supply the source that tells the machine what to do.
You can sample anything,
from fossils to the gum on your shoe...
To keep you from being bored,
there's nothing this machine won't do.
Strange Brew...
2 tons Smashed grapes!
????
Emily didn't know what she should do.
She needed tons of juice for her Strange Brew.
The she remembered her boots...
which took her back to her roots,
and the punks became the stompin' crew.
Strange Brew.

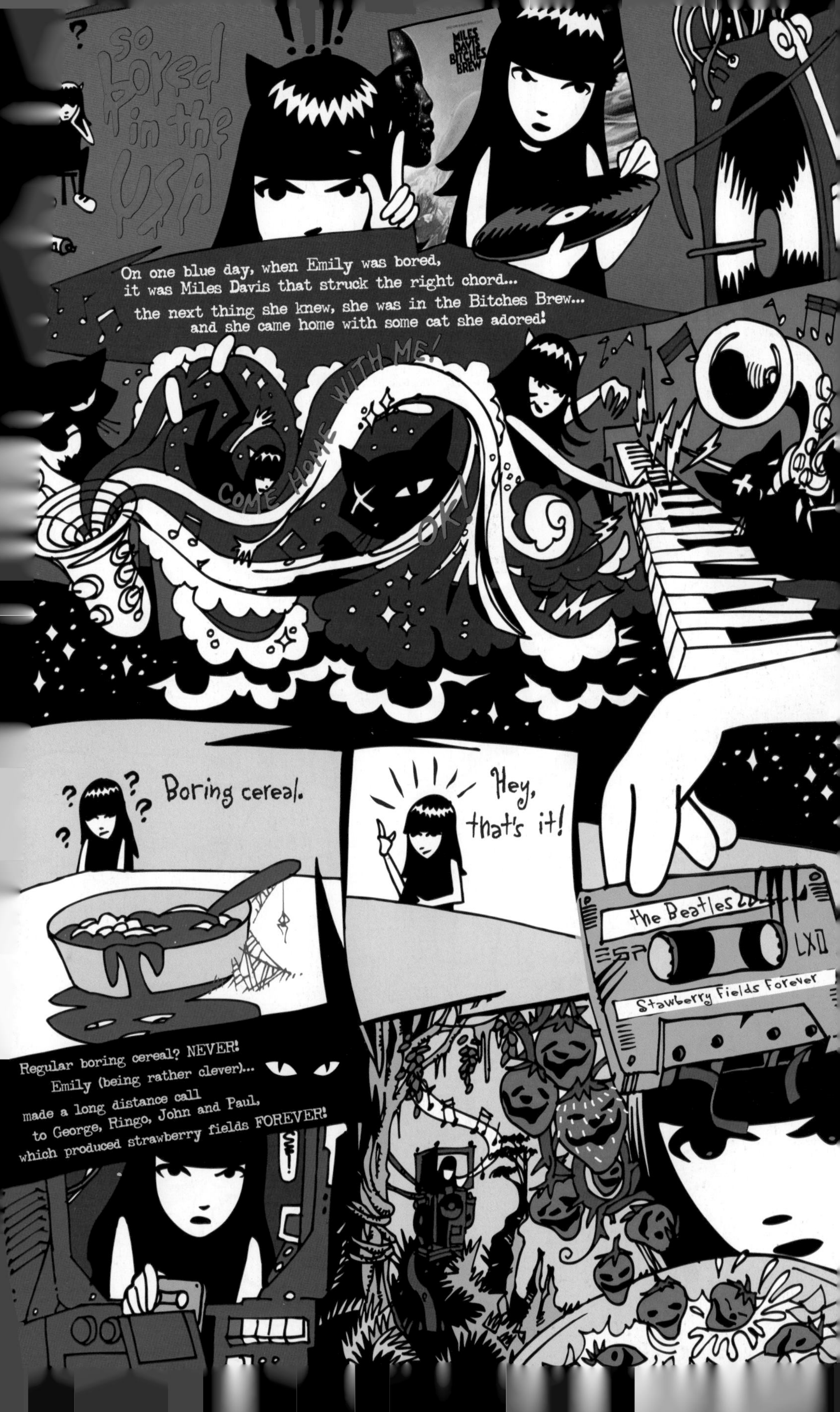
so bored in the USA
MILES DAVIS BITCHES BREW
On one blue day, when Emily was bored,
it was Miles Davis that struck the right chord...
the next thing she knew, she was in the Bitches Brew...
and she came home with some cat she adored!
COME HOME WITH ME!
OK!
Boring cereal.
Hey, that's it!
the Beatles
Stawberry Fields Forever
Regular boring cereal? NEVER!
Emily (being rather clever)...
made a long distance call
to George, Ringo, John and Paul,
which produced strawberry fields FOREVER!

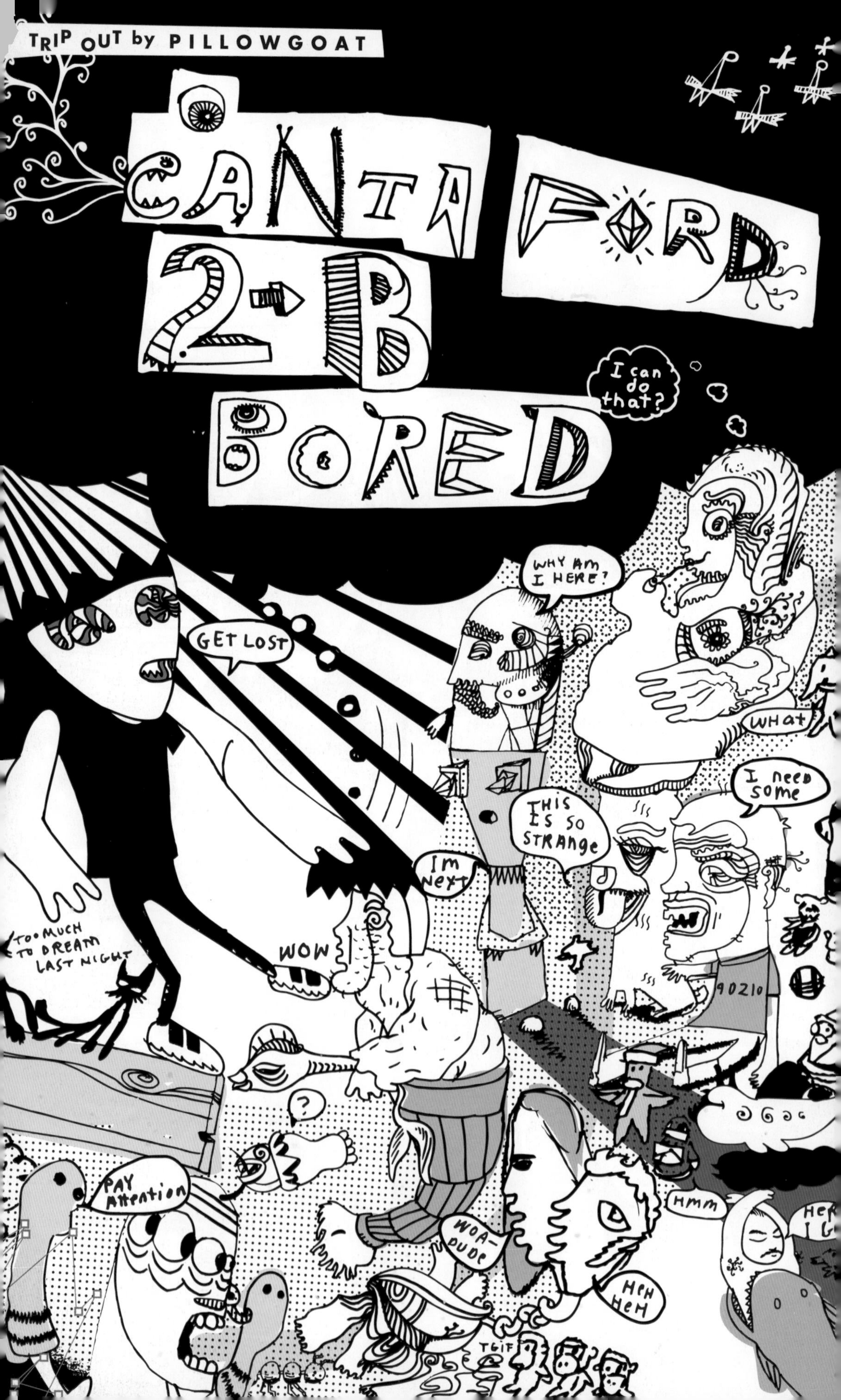
TRIP OUT by PILLOWGOAT
CANTA FORD
2 B
BORED
I can do that?
WHY AM I HERE?
GET LOST
WHAT
I need some
THIS IS SO STRANGE
IM NEXT
TOO MUCH TO DREAM LAST NIGHT
WOW
90210
?
PAY Attention
HMM
WOA-DUDE
HEH HEH
TGIF

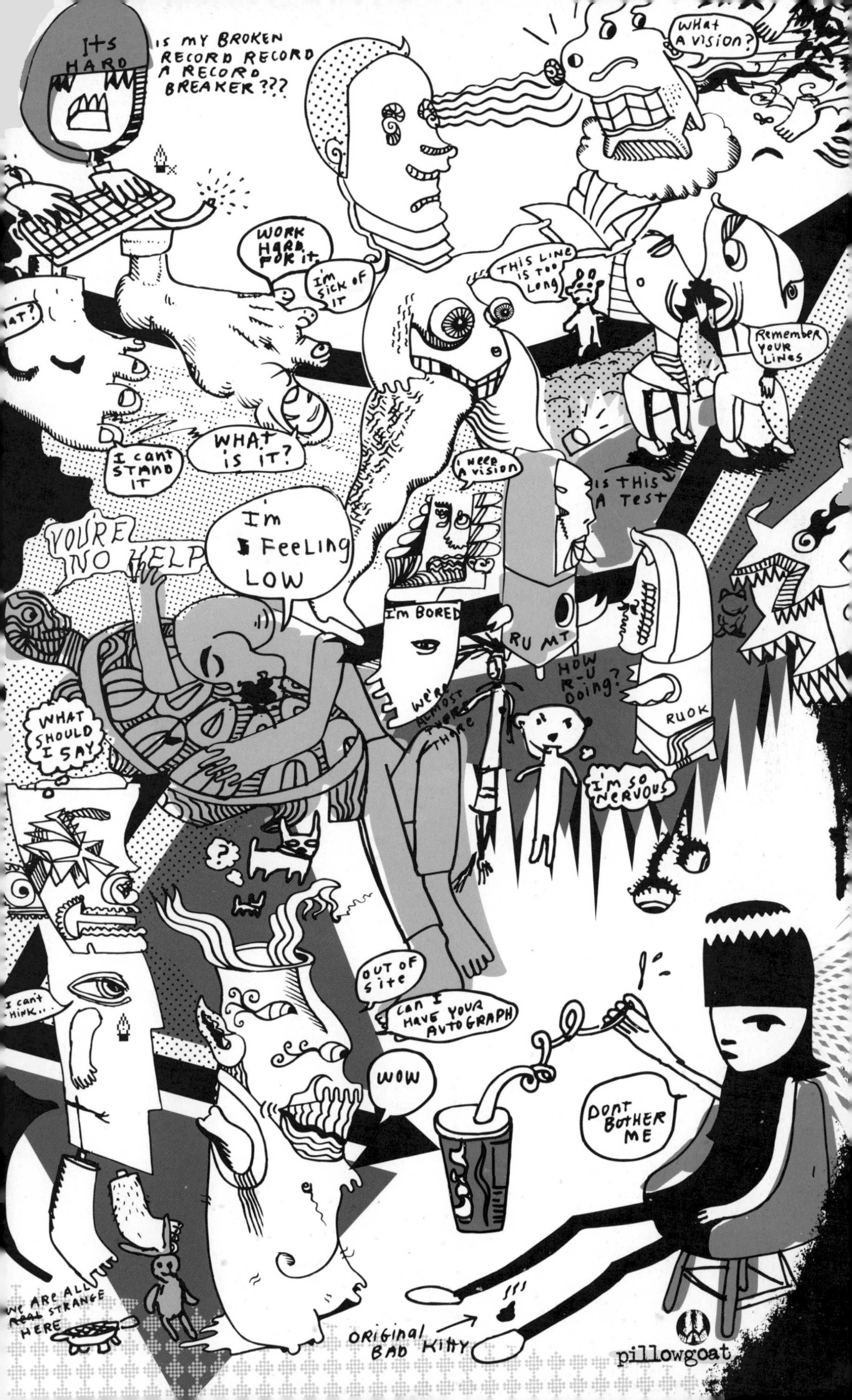

Its HARD
IS MY BROKEN RECORD RECORD A RECORD BREAKER???
WHAT A VISION?
WORK HARD FOR IT
I'M SICK OF IT
THIS LINE IS TOO LONG
REMEMBER YOUR LINES
WHAT IS IT?
I CANT STAND IT
I NEED A VISION
IS THIS A TEST
YOU'RE NO HELP
I'M FEELING LOW
I'M BORED
RU MT
HOW R-U DOING?
RUOK
WE'RE ALMOST THERE
WHAT SHOULD I SAY
I'M SO NERVOUS
OUT OF SITE
CAN I HAVE YOUR AUTOGRAPH
I can't hink..
WOW
DONT BOTHER ME
WE ARE ALL REAL STRANGE HERE
ORIGINAL BAD KITTY
pillowgoat

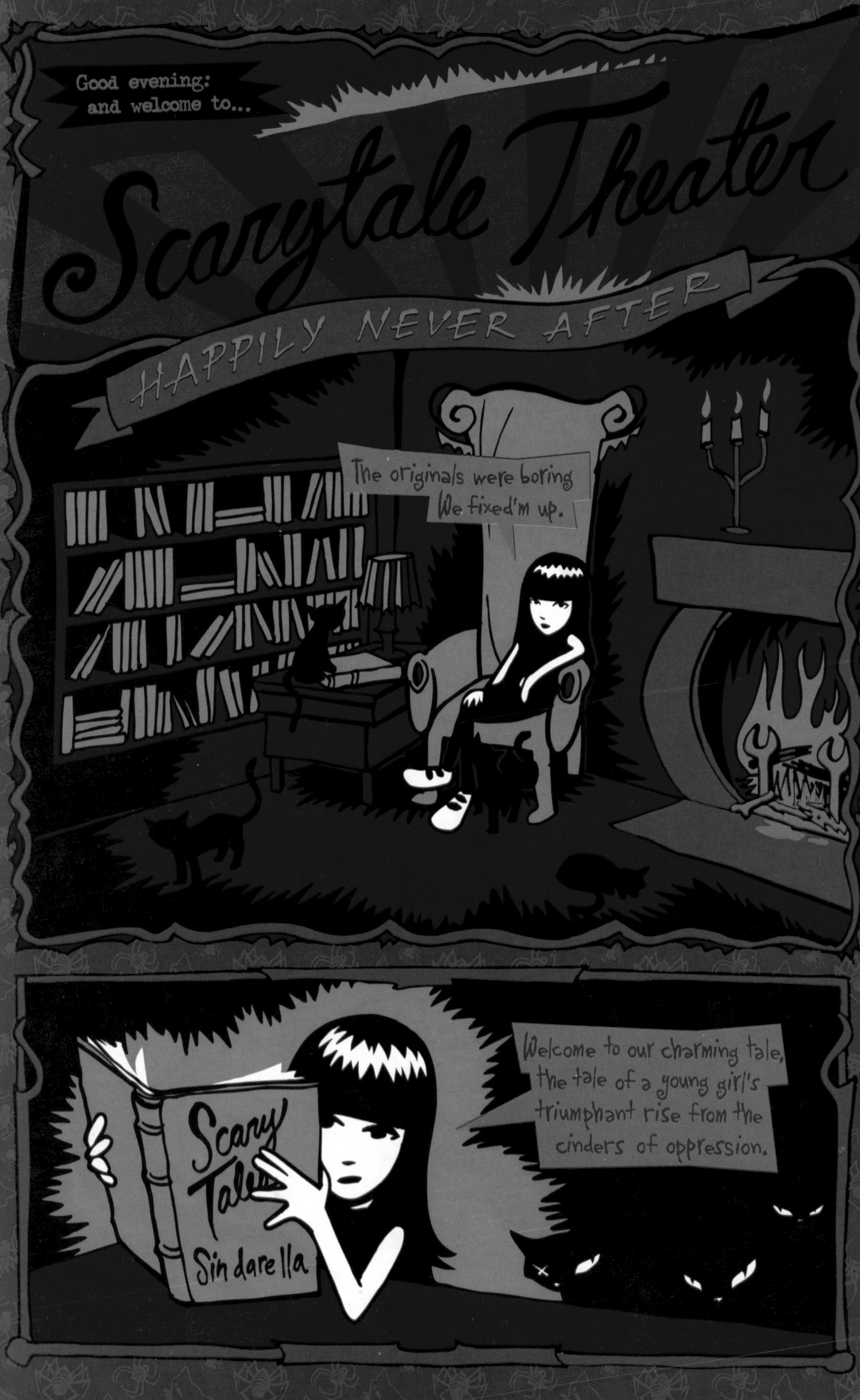
Good evening:
and welcome to...
Scarytale Theater
HAPPILY NEVER AFTER
The originals were boring
We fixed'm up.
Scary Tales
Sin darella
Welcome to our charming tale, the tale of a young girl's triumphant rise from the cinders of oppression.

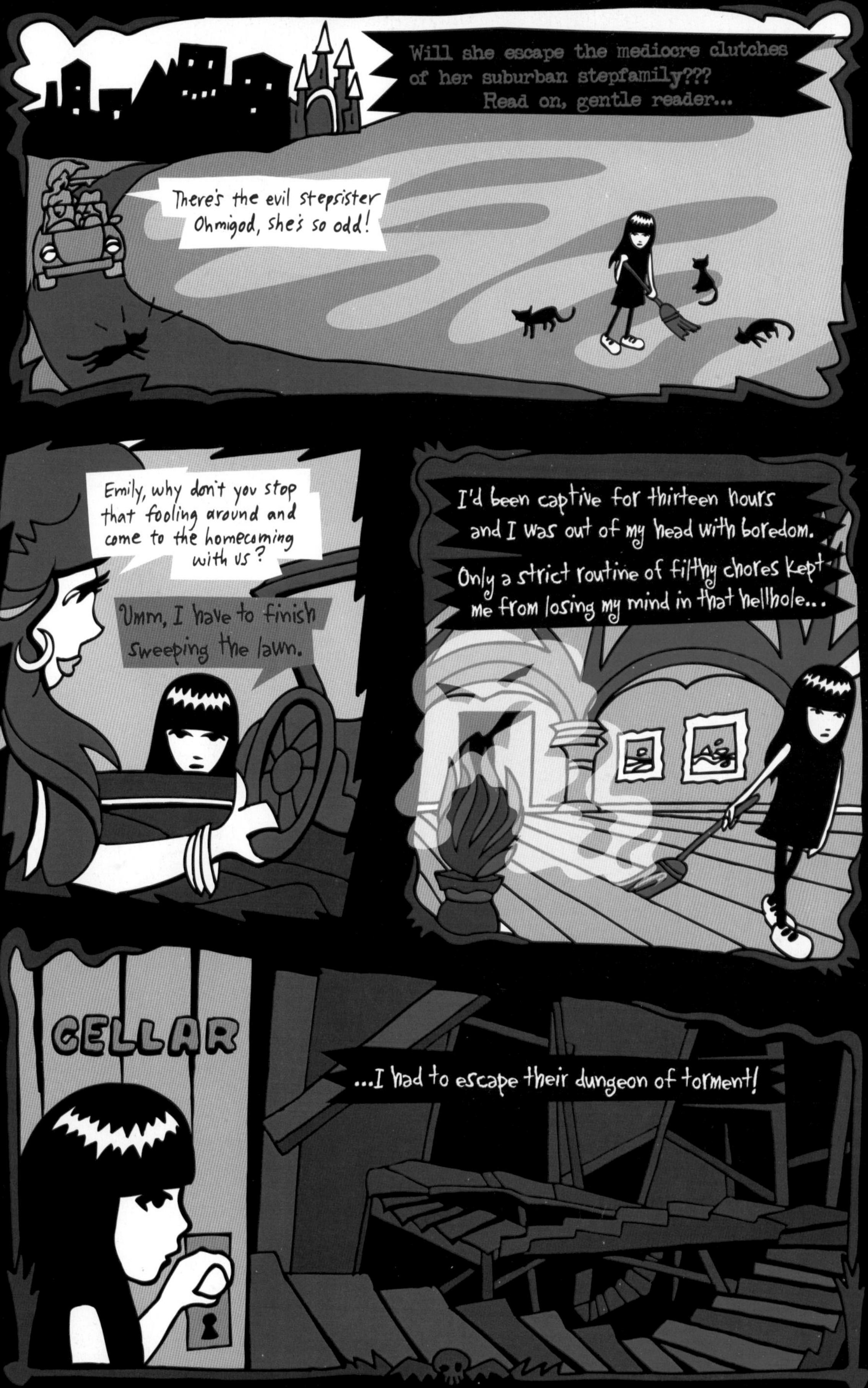
Will she escape the mediocre clutches of her suburban stepfamily??? Read on, gentle reader...
There's the evil stepsister Ohmigod, she's so odd!
Emily, why don't you stop that fooling around and come to the homecoming with us?
Umm, I have to finish sweeping the lawn.
I'd been captive for thirteen hours and I was out of my head with boredom.
Only a strict routine of filthy chores kept me from losing my mind in that hellhole...
CELLAR
...I had to escape their dungeon of torment!

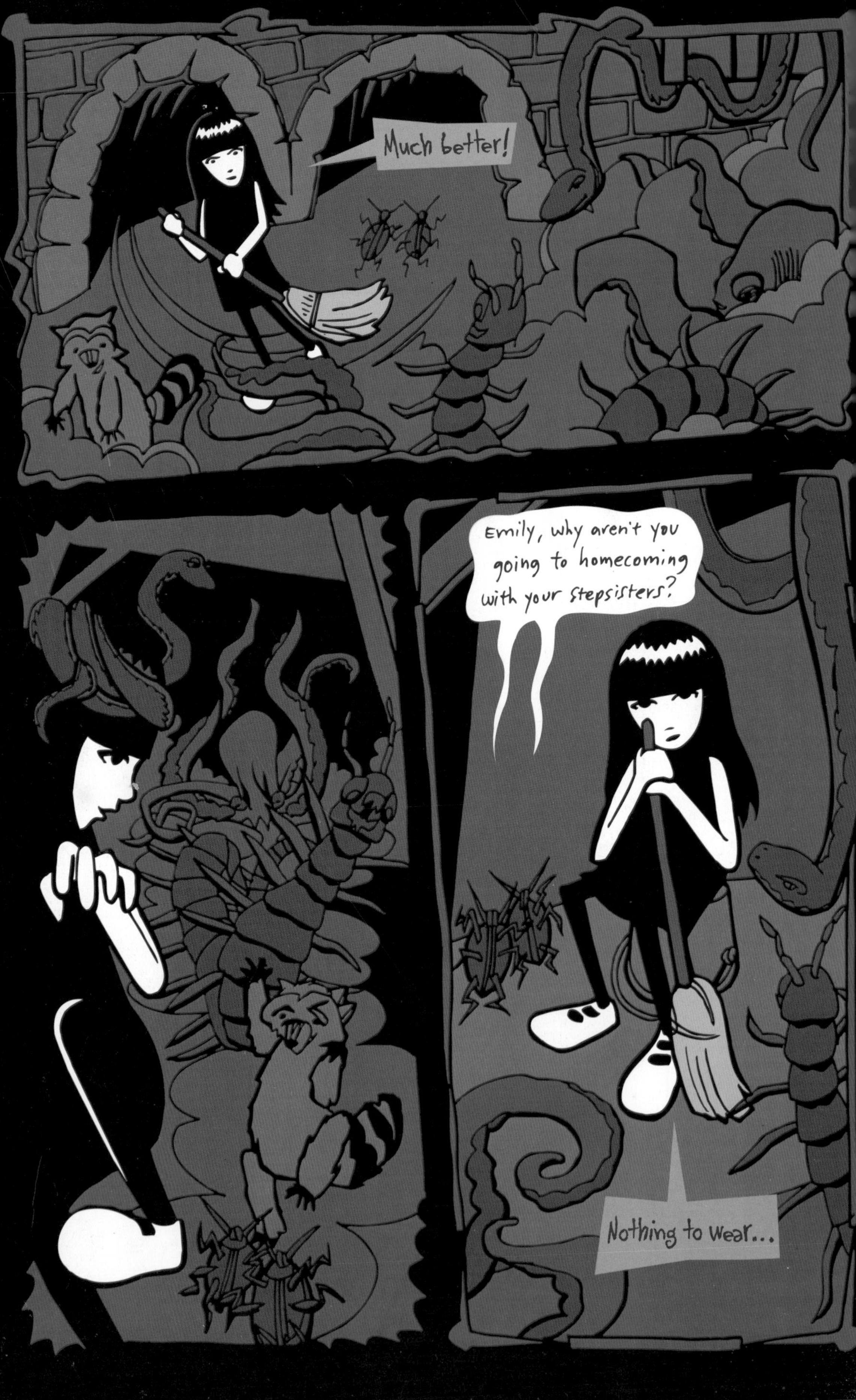
Much better!
Emily, why aren't you going to homecoming with your stepsisters?
Nothing to wear...

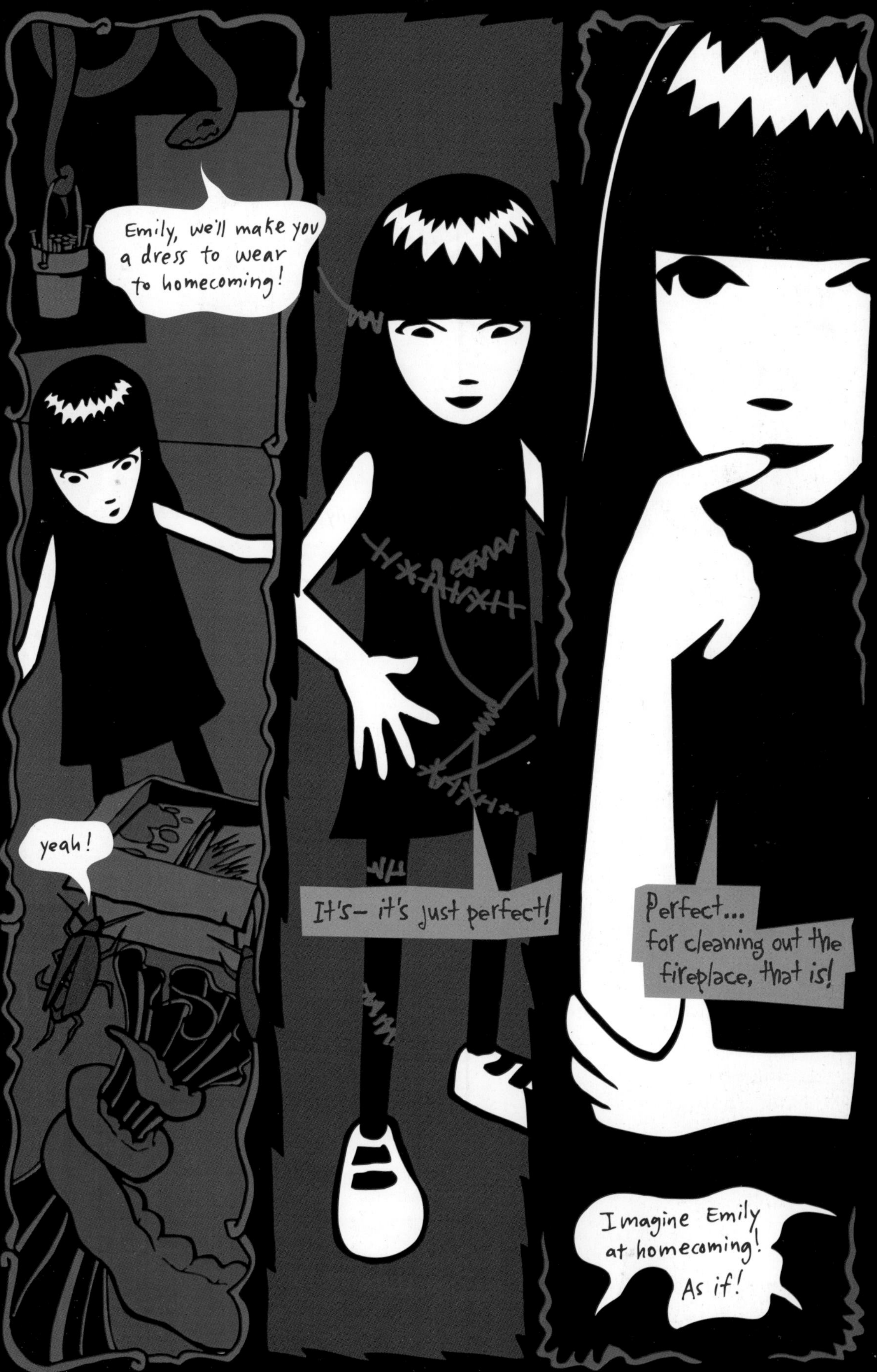
Emily, we'll make you a dress to wear to homecoming!
yeah!
It's– it's just perfect!
Perfect... for cleaning out the fireplace, that is!
Imagine Emily at homecoming! As if!

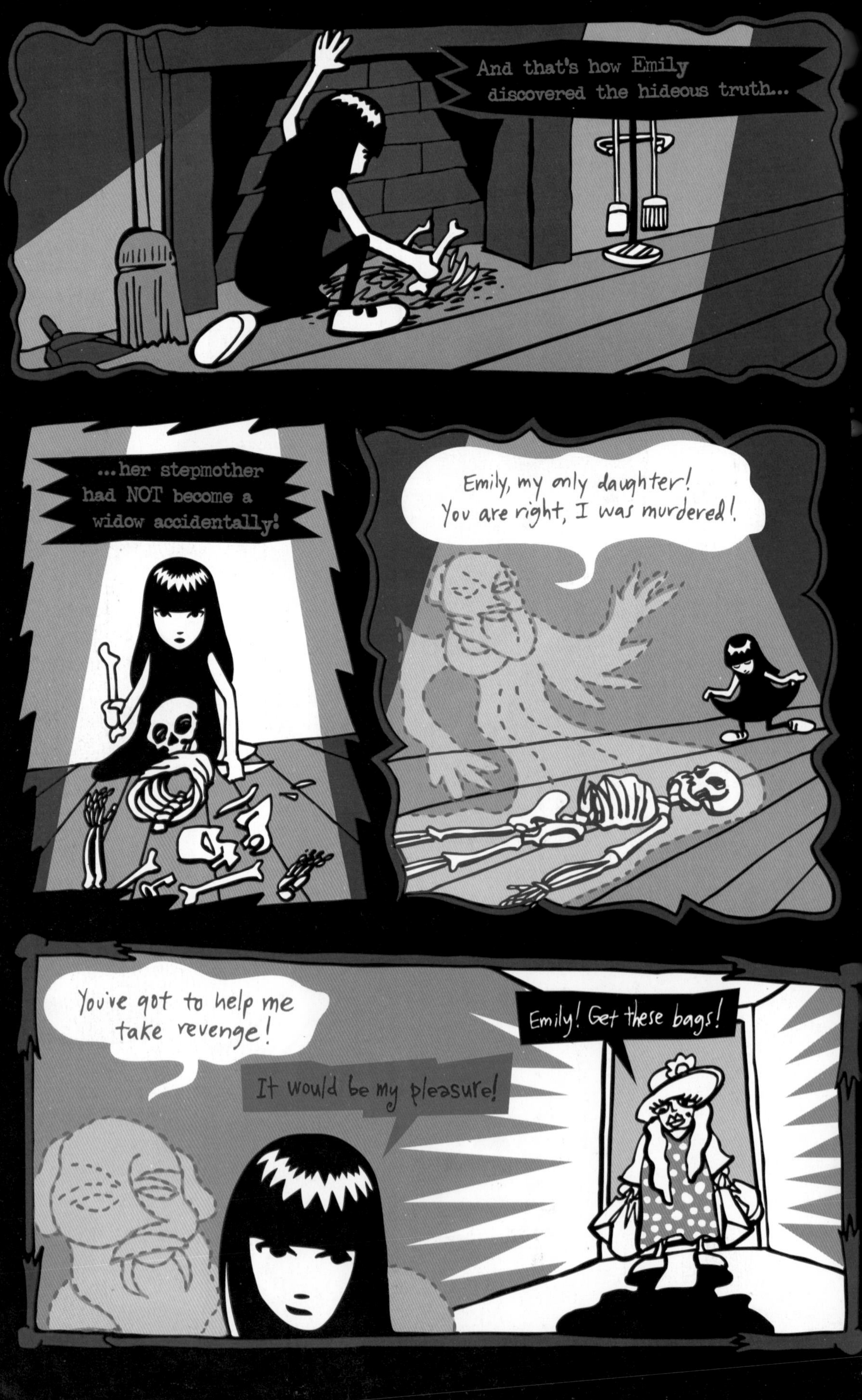
And that's how Emily discovered the hideous truth...
...her stepmother had NOT become a widow accidentally!
Emily, my only daughter! You are right, I was murdered!
You've got to help me take revenge!
It would be my pleasure!
Emily! Get these bags!

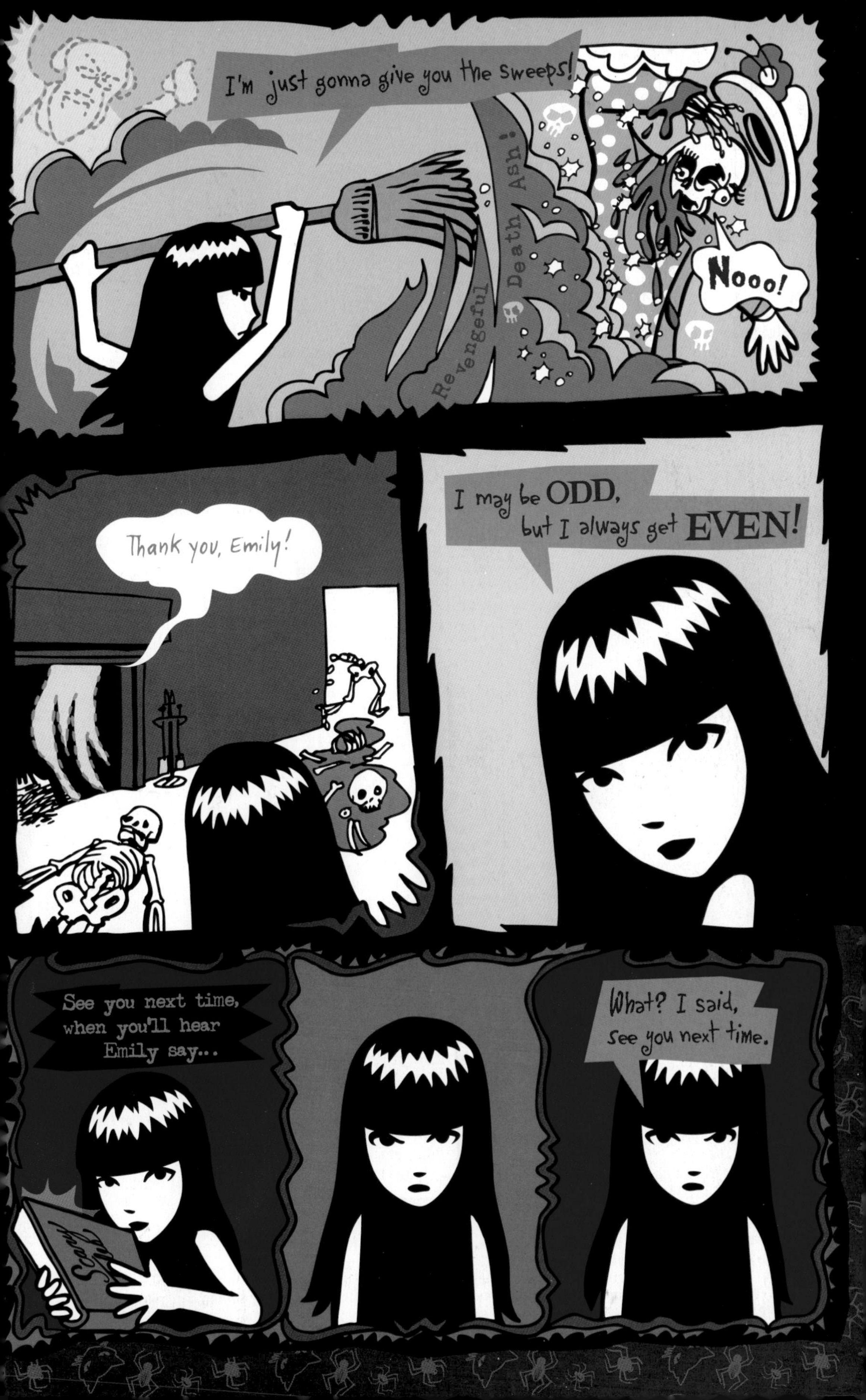

I'm just gonna give you the sweeps!
Revengeful Death Ash!
Nooo!
Thank you, Emily!
I may be ODD, but I always get EVEN!
See you next time, when you'll hear Emily say...
What? I said, see you next time.

Emily

Turn "Emily" upside down, and see something strange. For more useless word tricks, turn your wallet upside down & send us your money!

No.1319. . . . . $ 13.00

Lazy? Sick? Bored?

I bet you ARE! There's nothing wrong with that... More for the rest of us to do! In fact, in our detailed informational booklet, you can easily learn how to let the rest of us do ALL OF YOUR stinking work.

How to Let Us Get Ahead While You Sleep
No. 1365. . . . . 75¢

Paint It Black Kit

Paint unwanted obnoxiously colored bright goodies all black. Achieve the entire spectrum! Get back in black and color me BAD!

Paint it Black Kit
No. 1348 . . . . .$25

FAKE BLOOD!

really you don't need this- you should have plenty of the real stuff! Turn your boring self into something worth looking at!

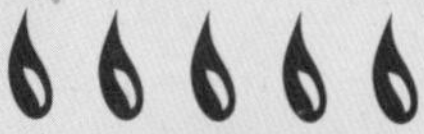

From BORE to GORE
No. 66. . . . . . $2.13

ARE YOU UGLY?

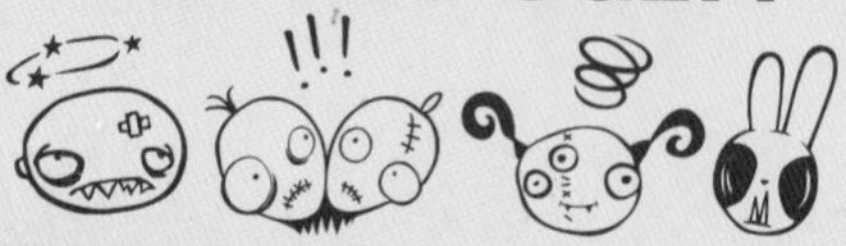

YEAH, we know. Luckily, NOW it's OK to be ugly! Find out 100 exciting ways your life is better because you **are** ugly! There are more of us ugly mothers than them!

Ugly or NOT, You STINK!
No. 1311. . . . . $4.95

FRIEND OR FOE?

Change your 'friends' to 'FIENDS' with this Magic Marker!

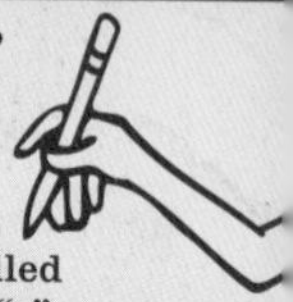

Grab hold of any so-called "friend" and cross out their "r", with our "magic" marker and make them a "FIEND!"

No. 209 Crossin' Fools Out! $9.75

SNORING POTION

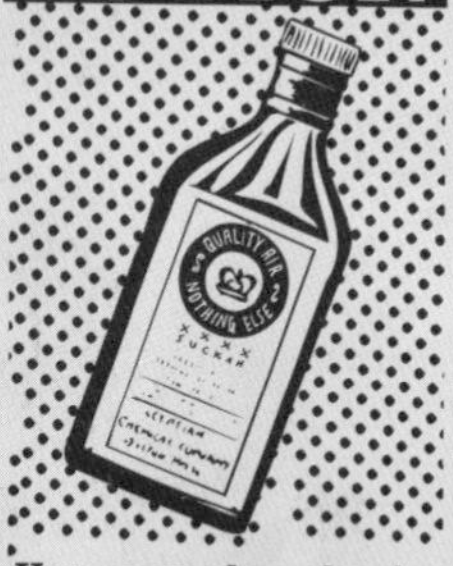

You ever heard of... "boring, boring, the old man is snoring"? Well you will now! One dose and the comatose will rock your world...

Nothing But Air.
No. 1384. . . . . . .$18

STRANGE SAUCE

Food Loaf getting you down? Let your inner bug out! A few drops of this tincture and your HEAD will explode! (not to worry- you probably won't miss it)

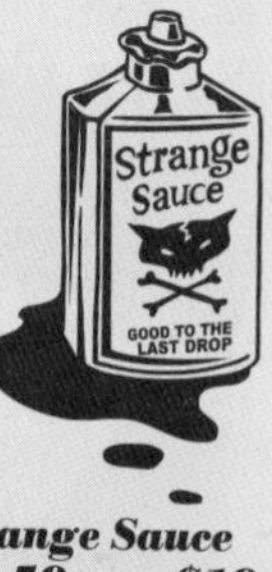
Strange Sauce
GOOD TO THE LAST DROP

Strange Sauce
No. 59. . . . .$19.95

ARE YOU BORING?

YEAH, we know you are. Luckily, NOW it's not only OK to be boring, it's the best way to get promoted! You can be Chairman of the Bored in 3 short weeks! Life is better the more your bored...

ZZZZZZZ

Another Boring Idea
2158. . . . . $2.80

THINK HARD

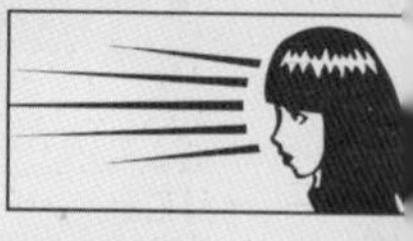

Strengthen your mind with just a few daily exercises! A full instructional booklet will have you thinking in days!

Cross Word Puzzles
No.1355. . . . . . $95

X-RAY VISION

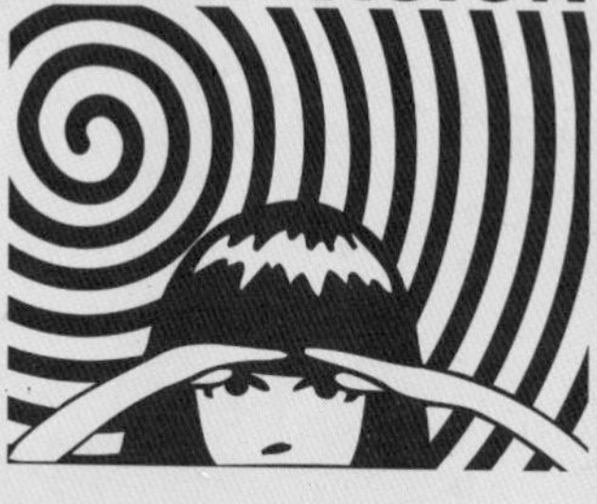

"I can see right through you. . . It's like you aren't even there!" -Emily

Simple Surgery
No. 13205. . . . . $7.25
w/out insurance
No. 13255. . . . .$42,358

SHADOW BOXING

You're in the spotlight, and don't know what to do... Flash a gang signal, give the bird, or learn many "cool" shadow tricks.

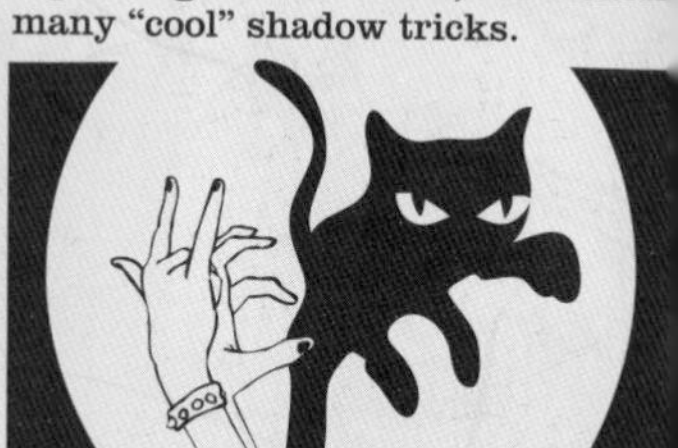

Shady Ideas
No. 1340. . . . . $3.95
w/ coupon for manicure
No. 1341. . . . . $32.35

ABSOLUTLY NOTHING

Absolutely Nothing (includes Shipping)
No. 00. . . . .$2.95

NEEDLE IN THE HAY

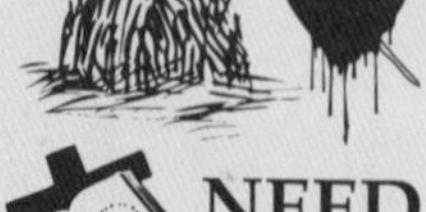

Need something that you can't seem to find? Keep looking-

No. 1021. . . . . . .$3

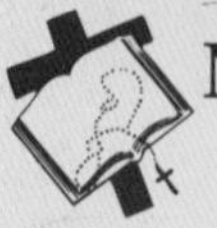

NEED A NEW RELIGION?

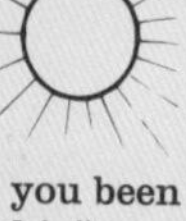

Tired of your boring Religion? Have you been caught falling asleep during "worship" one too many times? Maybe you need a NEW Religion! The most popular ones aren't always the best... Our good book will help you set up a Religion of your very own! Be a priest, bishop, pope, or witch for all we care! Or choose from the many strange whacko religions we have already set up for you to join.

Change of religion
No. 1366. . . . .$8.50

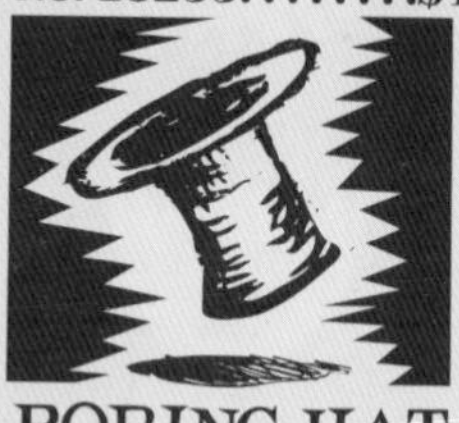

BORING HAT

Ever need something that you ain't got? Get your hands on one of these beauties and you'll ain't never need nothing else!

No. 1315. . . . . . . $ 75

LIE DETECTOR

FREE TRUSTWORTHY ADVICE
We'll let you in on a little secret... It's ALL lies! That's right, you thought they were telling you the honest truth, but the truth is, they are lying through their rotten teeth. Really... no lie!

Free Advice No. 1369 . . . . $2.25

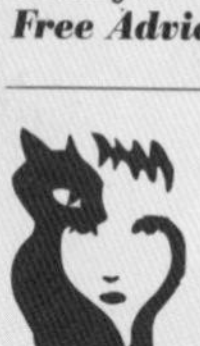

So artistic we're almost autistic - but always authentic... Look no further.

Give us a shout!

COSMIC DEBRIS

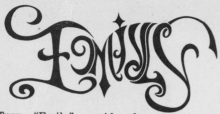

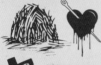